THUNDER GODS GOLD

"Traditions are those intimate glimpses of history too personal to their makers, too unbelievable to anyone else, to be recorded like more normal occurrences."

— JAY C. HENSON

Barry Storm is himself an expert prospector and confirmed treasure hunter.[2]

"What is history but a fable agreed upon?"
— Napoleon

THUNDER GODS GOLD

by BARRY STORM

THE AMAZING TRUE STORY OF AMERICA'S
MOST FAMED LOST GOLD MINES, EPITOME OF
WESTERN TRADITIONS.

EPBM

ECHO POINT BOOKS & MEDIA, LLC
Brattleboro, Vermont

To The Prospector

Whose Daring Enterprise On Lonely Trails
Has Built And Will Forever Sustain The
Destiny Of A Metallic Civilization, Thunder
Gods Gold, His Timeless Dream,

Is Dedicated

Published in 2020 by Echo Point Books & Media
Brattleboro, Vermont
www.EchoPointBooks.com

Originally published in 1945 by Treasure Trail Edition.

Thunder God's Gold
ISBN: 978-1-63561-867-9 (casebound)
978-1-63561-868-6 (paperback)

Cover design by Kaitlyn Whitaker

CONTENTS WITH ILLUSTRATIONS

Note: Superior numbers in text and cutlines refer to Notes Of Authenticity, which see.

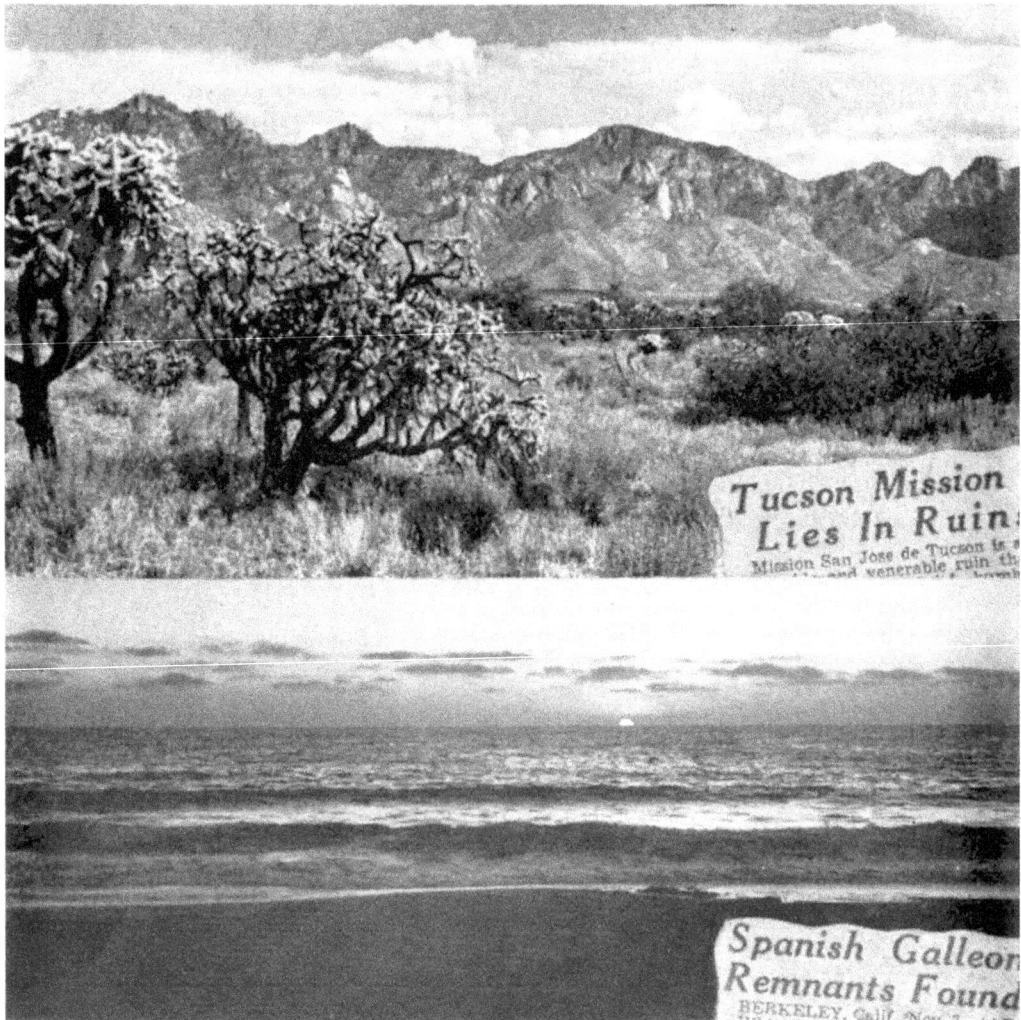

By land and sea into uncharted Western wilds many generations of adventurers explored after the virgin mineral wealth which now is phantom tradition.

PART I

WESTERN TREASURELAND

"There are more things in heaven and earth, Horatio, than are dreamed of in your philosophy."
— SHAKESPEARE

Lost Wheelbarrow Mine Re-Discovered

Marvelous Ore Lies Buried Near Pyramid

Lost Spanish Mine Found

Fabulous Colorado Gold Legend Stirs 300-Year Search

Dutch Oven Mine

BARRY STORM WILL LEAD SEEKERS FOR LOST ARIZONA ORE

Old Spanish Workings in Superstition Mountains Found in Cliff by Prospectors

Electric Prospecting De-

Clue to Lost Adams Diggins . . . Rowood, Arizona

Dear Desert:

LOST COPPER MINE IN ARIZONA FOUND

In the turbulent backwash of centuries since California was thought to be an island[1] rich mineral lodes were found and abandoned, bonanza mines lost, treasure troves buried. Today, fabulous headlines[2] often prove the truth of Western traditions!

I. IN TREASURELAND

More than four centuries ago the first bearded adventurer set foot upon a wild, new world in a frenzied search for gold. And hard upon his trail came sanguine thousands of every race and color who marched and countermarched through incredible, high-handed treasure hunts. Today in the vast, fabulous reaches of our American West the daring ones are marching still not only after new mineral wealth but after, too, all those golden promises of hidden mines and treasure troves long since lost in the turbulent backwash of time!

And there are clues for the hardy, roseate visions for dreamers. For endlessly with each fresh sigh of the nightwind there come vague whisperings of half-remembered tales and exciting traditions which somehow fall just short of being accredited history or discredited legend, traditions of all those phantom bonanzas forever hidden beyond the purple horizon mists—yet, strangely, nowadays occasionally refound!

Refound like one of the eight Lost Peralta Mines[3] in Arizona, the Lost Wheelbarrow Mine[2] in Idaho, a covered Spanish shaft[2] in high Colorado and vast, unrecorded workings[2] in Nevada, like the Lost Padre[4] in California long since secretly gutted of its gold or the Santa Rita[5] in New Mexico still a producing mine. And with hidden hordes of treasure too like the seven muleloads of phantom bullion[6] drifting wraith-like over a full dozen states or the buried Spanish smelters in the mission-yard of Tumacacori[7] actually found stuffed with gold, silver and copper ingots!

Indeed, the adventures of a Coronado[8] who found nothing save mud huts and skulking savages in 1541 or of an Espejo[8] who discovered gold mines in 1852 are well enough chronicled. But what of those uncounted others who trekked into unexplored wilds and prospected, mined or looted there as opportunity offered? Sometimes we hear of them by chance when an ancient treasure map comes to light among the heirlooms of some pioneer family, when an **antigua** mine is suddenly stumbled upon where no mine had been known, when the cabalistic lettering of explorer-priests or the mysterious treasure signs of long forgotten miners are found cut into rock, trees, cacti. And what human can sleep soundly beneath Western stars when the subtle jingle of lost gold rings so persistently over the land!

If then the first flaming facts of Cortes' fantastic plunder,[9] of the fabulous mines of **Tayopa**[10] and **Gloria Pan,**[11] of the incredible riches of **Nueva Grenada** stampeded the Old World, the more recent, equally as fantastic facts of California and Colorado gold[12] could hardly be blamed for stampeding the New. Nor was it long before Nevada silver had stampeded both, and Arizona copper had stampeded Nevada.[13] And all the lessor but equally as exciting facts[2] before and since of bonanza lodes found, lost, rediscovered and hidden—and the secret treasures each had produced!—will forever exemplify in those wide, frontier lands dreams as paradoxically old as time itself yet as perpetually new as tomorrow's golden dawn.

That eternal, ever-recurring vision was set forth in these exquisite words by Casteñeda[8] who recorded Coronado's sanguine hunt for a Seven Golden Cities Of Cibola: "Granted that they did not find the riches of which they had been told, they found a place in which to search for them."

And that place is still there with its ever-accumulating traditions of long lost treasure trails to be heard about in every crossroad tavern and village store, in every cow-camp and mining town and wherever desert dust and mountain haze obscures still-wild distance. That place is still largely a raw, rugged land of endless plains, wide deserts, towering mountains and twisted canyon-chasms. Such ground can never be plowed under for it is too vast, too primeval, too hot or cold or remote. So the wild countryside preserves its treasures well and has given to the whole of America an exciting folklore, a strange flavor from more spacious ages, peculiarly its own.

In fact, when Gonzales,[14] the last of the Peralta descendents, passed on to his American friend, Erwin C. Ruth,[15] in 1912 an heirloom map to mines once worked in Arizona by his ancestors he merely perpetuated the timeless dream. For if one wanted fortune, one simply set out to find it. If one didn't need fortune, well, couldn't one search anyway?

The adventurer always has little which he accounts of as much value as Adventure. The adventurer always has sublime dreams to discredit fear and mock disaster. And so long as phantom gold—his modern allegory of every misty mirage ever pursued by the high heart of man—is somewhere else, anywhere else, he can seek it with an undying faith. But let the gold be found or the treasure counted then gone forever in the fears of possession is an essential way of life that is peculiarly American, a way of life built entirely upon individual achievement, **the** way of life that has constructed a new world, launched fleets, moved mountains, migrated populations, conquered frontiers. **Thunder Gods Gold** is of all this compact, epitome of the fabulous fabric of dreams that forever will blend over wild Western lands the romantic flavor of many centuries, many peoples, many traditions.

And if it would seem that these traditions of hidden wealth and boundless treasure all have a certain family resemblance, it must be remembered that there was—and is! —a resemblance too in the remote wilderness of Spaniard and American alike—and thereby in the usual causes of disaster. For disaster, in one word, has ever been the story of phantom bonanzas, has always occurred to hide the missing link on a return trail to once-found fabulous mineral wealth. Indeed, had not someone been killed, had not time erased memories or confused directions, had not wars, politics, accident or human greed intervened there would be today none of the hidden tunnels, abandoned lodes or treasures in already-mined riches which are accidently stumbled upon or purposely sought and occasionally refound.[2] And because Spanish miner and American prospector alike were working virgin ground first it was invariably the largest lode present that was left, the richest vein that was hidden—phantom mines which usually and quite logically were real bonanzas.[2]

Occasionally the traditions of these bonanzas had been recorded in great and exact detail by their original discoverers. But far more often they are as intangible as the drifting morning mists because of understandable and very human reasons; because crime had been committed or tax or tithe evaded, because traveling in possession of a known fortune was dangerous or because someone might one day wish to return to its source, because once fortune was obtained at great hazard it was easier and far safer to simply walk off from its source rather than encounter the necessity for explanations to jealous men and greedy governments. Yet, whether whispered tradition or authenticated fact, such little-known, almost incredible history[7] speaks loudly in every Western community in support of a universal theme common to all peoples and all climes. It is a theme most peculiar to a new world in which the minds of men were attuned to the individual pursuit of fortune and of adventure and not that of woman, a theme part and parcel of the westward course of empire, of the sanguine ventures of the frontiersmen and pioneers who pushed ever further into uncharted wilds. Virgin gold or lost gold, furs, free lands, cattle and gushing oil are all one, the lure of adventurous achievement which drew the self-sufficient, individualistic men of the flaming times of the Spanish and Western American conquests into hazardous, irrational deeds by our sophisticated standards but only because of essential motivations and human characteristics which are now fast ceasing to exist in the modern, group-controlled quagmire of cattle-like human herds.

Such unorthodox history then is not important because of its actors or locale but because it epitomizes in even this more romantic aspect to the outer ramparts of a continent the dreams and deeds, the daring, ingenuity and achievements once allowed by personal enterprise, because it is history which revolved wholely around the singular motive of individual reward for daring individual effort which alone constructed a new world, because it is tradition rooted deep in the soil which hides even buried treasures and covers even lost mines—those magic lures which are still capable of crystallizing so many human weaknesses and human strengths into glorious purpose! For venerated alike by the romantic past and wishful present ever since the day Jason set sail after his Golden Fleece treasure trove has always been the fabulous touchstone of Desire, the eternal dream of personal Destiny, the wish-fulfillment of Vanity, the muted hope of tremendous Achievement at one bold stroke.

Nor does this bonanza history belong alone to romantic centuries and forgotten generations. In the mineralized West it is still-living history,[16] occurs again and again today and will continue to repeat its fabulous tale so long as there are adventurous men to seek wealth in the ground or an ever-expanding metallic civilization which has desperate need of minerals upon which to grow. Indeed, it was only a few years ago that Jack McDaniels,[16] who supplied many New York jewelers with their amethyst, stumbled upon a rich ledge of brown quartz gold ore on the way to his amethyst crystal mine in Arizona, actually built a mile of trail toward it in preparing to move down, then went into Globe for supplies only to be burned to death in a hotel fire the very night of his arrival—and before he could record the bonanza location. But not before he had generously passed out samples of the fantastic, new-found ore on his way to town! And scores in every Western state like Durkin[2] of Nevada and Schofield[2] of California have their fabulous and well-authenticated but seldom refound lodes.

How many of these phantom mines or bonanza veins—and the treasures many of them have produced!—lost now for a decade or a century or two or merely since day before yesterday could be again "discovered" either accidently or by purposeful search? No one perhaps can truthfully guess—though that same roseate dream is as much a part of the eternally primeval West as its far-flung plains, bottomless deserts and vast mountain slopes and of those people there who have not yet lost in the mediocre ways of the human herd[17] their individual capacity to dare adventure their dreams into fabulous reality.

Then how many such treasures in mineral wealth "lost" during a vanished era have really been found? The number must be vast if the half-whispered tales common to every Western community of someone's sudden affluence, of a mine opened and gutted of its ore where no mine had before been, of mysterious holes left gaping open, can be only half believed. But the number of them is always unknown for various personal reasons of the finders, and usually because it is not expedient, today more than ever, to allow jealous men and the governments which reflect their mass greed[17] to learn the truth, a legitimate enough reason to individualistic people who gain what they have by daring initiative and hazardous personal enterprise at no expense to the unthinking human masses who would steal the results of their labors by sheer political weight of numbers. And yet, in addition and in the last few years alone the public discovery[2] of a dozen or more lost bonanza mines of considerable wealth have already written as many exciting headlines!

Who is there then who can doubt the veritable golden promise in all the "traditional" treasure trails left behind during a more gallant age by those daring ones who will live forever on in desert dust and mountain haze, who spring to life anew with each fresh whisper of free winds blowing . . .

2. GOLDEN TRAILS

La Sombrera or Weaver's Needle in the wild Superstitions beckons still with alluring promise.[18] But beware else it shall look down too upon your bleaching bones!

to Fort
McDowel

Bagley Flat

RIO
SALADO

Apache Gap

Mormon Flat

Geronimo
Head

Garden
Valley

MARICOPA CO.
PINAL CO.

Black
Mesa

Goldfield

to Apache
Junction, Mesa,
Phoenix

SUPERSTITION MOUNTAINS

N A T I O N A L

Bluff
Sp. Mt.

Weavers
Needle

Picacho
Butte

Miner's
Needle

Barke
Ranch

BASE

MAGNETIC NORTH
DECLINATIONS EAST

year 1944: 14° 16'
year 1847: 12° 58'

Scale

5 Miles

5 Kilometers

Contour interval 100 feet.

T O N T O

to Pinal
Florence
Tucson

Jenkins
gold ore
trail

Walz
placer
gold

Storm
gold

Military
Trail

Reid
gold
ore

mule
shoe

Ruth
site

signs
and
map

camp,
etc. of
Dutchman

on Peralta Mt.

charcoal
pit

Wiser's
cached
articles

soldiers
shell

Peralta
key
marker

Apache
marker

Peralta
camp

Charle-
bois
canyon

Peralta
master
map

Peralta
mine

Wiser's
trail

Howland
gold on
Wagoner
trail

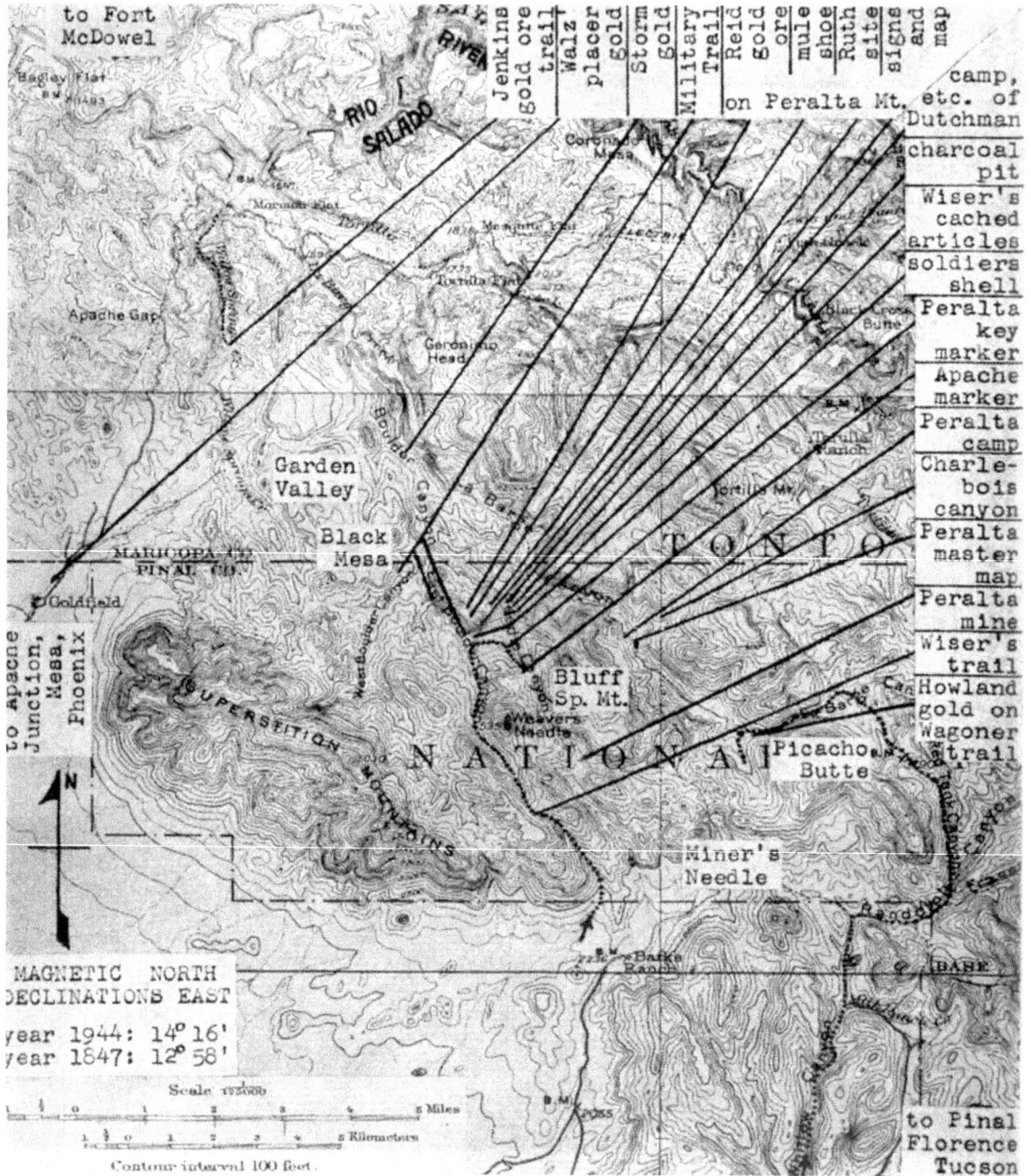

Topographic map of the Superstitions showing the locations of lost mine clues.[18]

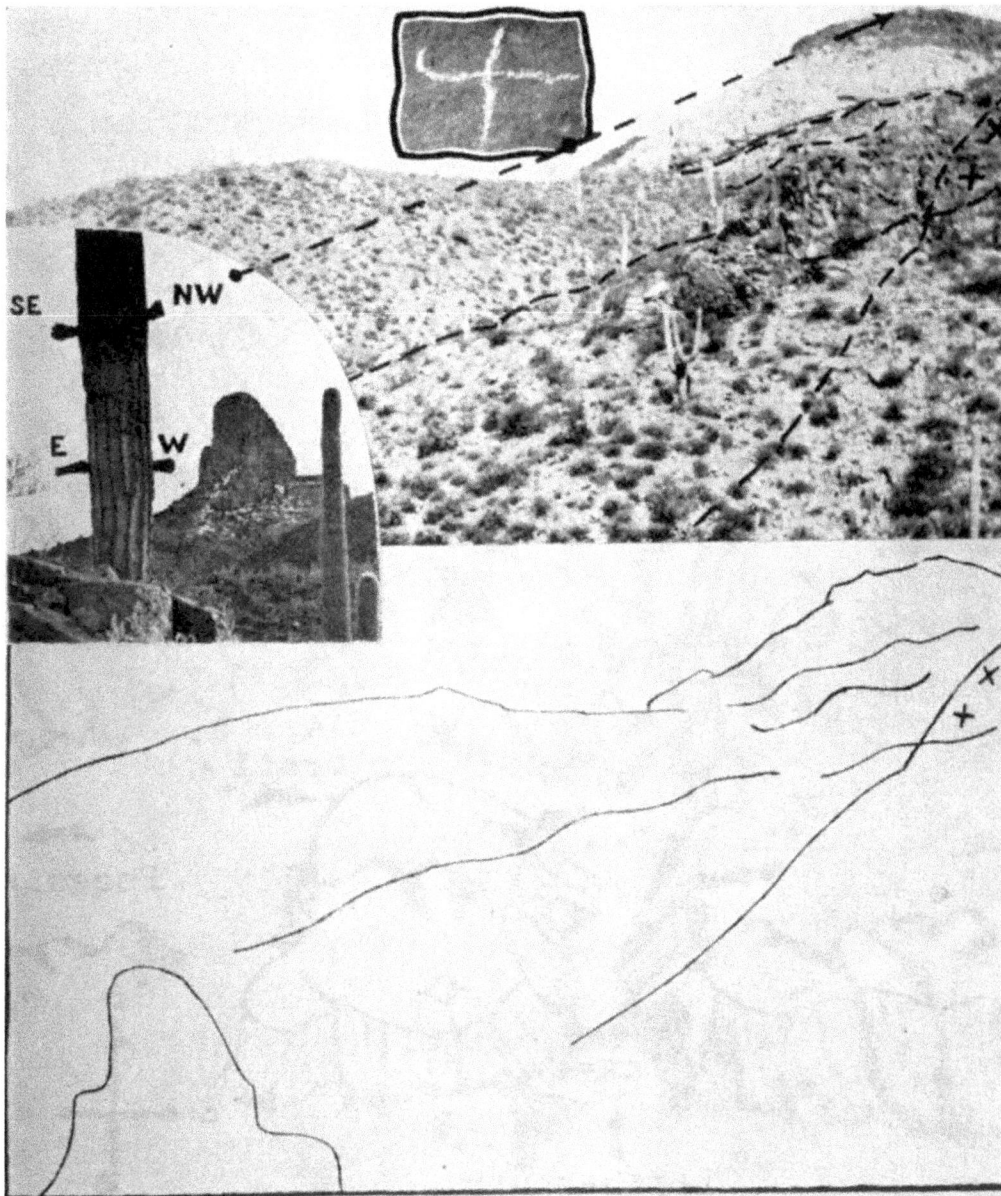

The Peralta-mapped mountain[19] photographed from Pedro's (large inset) key marker[33] in Needle Canyon from which **La Sombrera**[21] beyond and (super-imposed lines) the mapped mountain **both** match in topographic outlines from **different** directions the Peralta map[20] below. Stones inserted in the giant saguaro point by compass declination for the year 1848[34] northwest (dotted line) to (top inset) Spanish signs (arrow) atop the mapped mountain, east to a master map and southeast and west to something unknown.[35] Do crosses locate the way to gold?

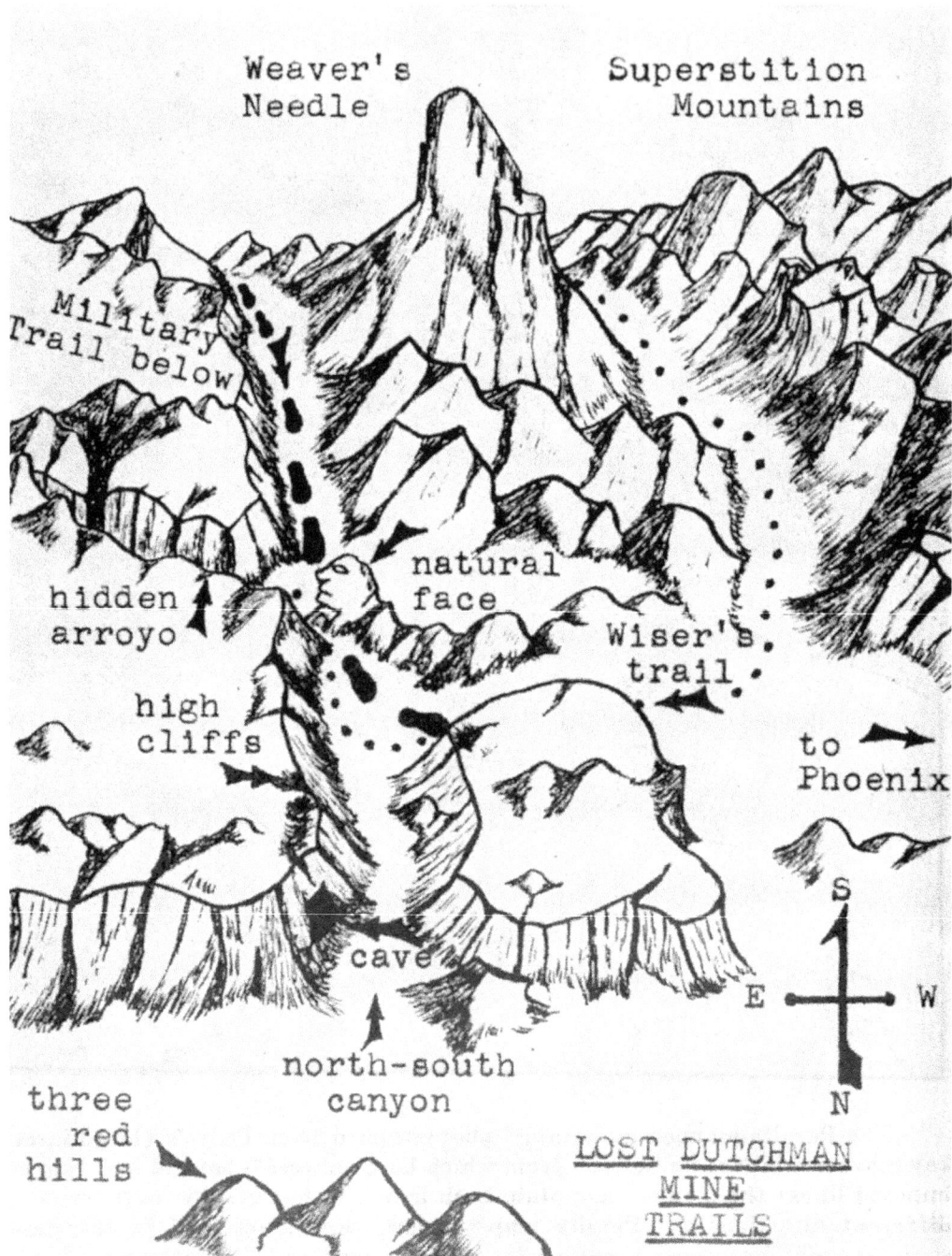

The Dutchman's lost mine map,[22] modernized to show the location clues about which he told and Wiser's trail.[23]

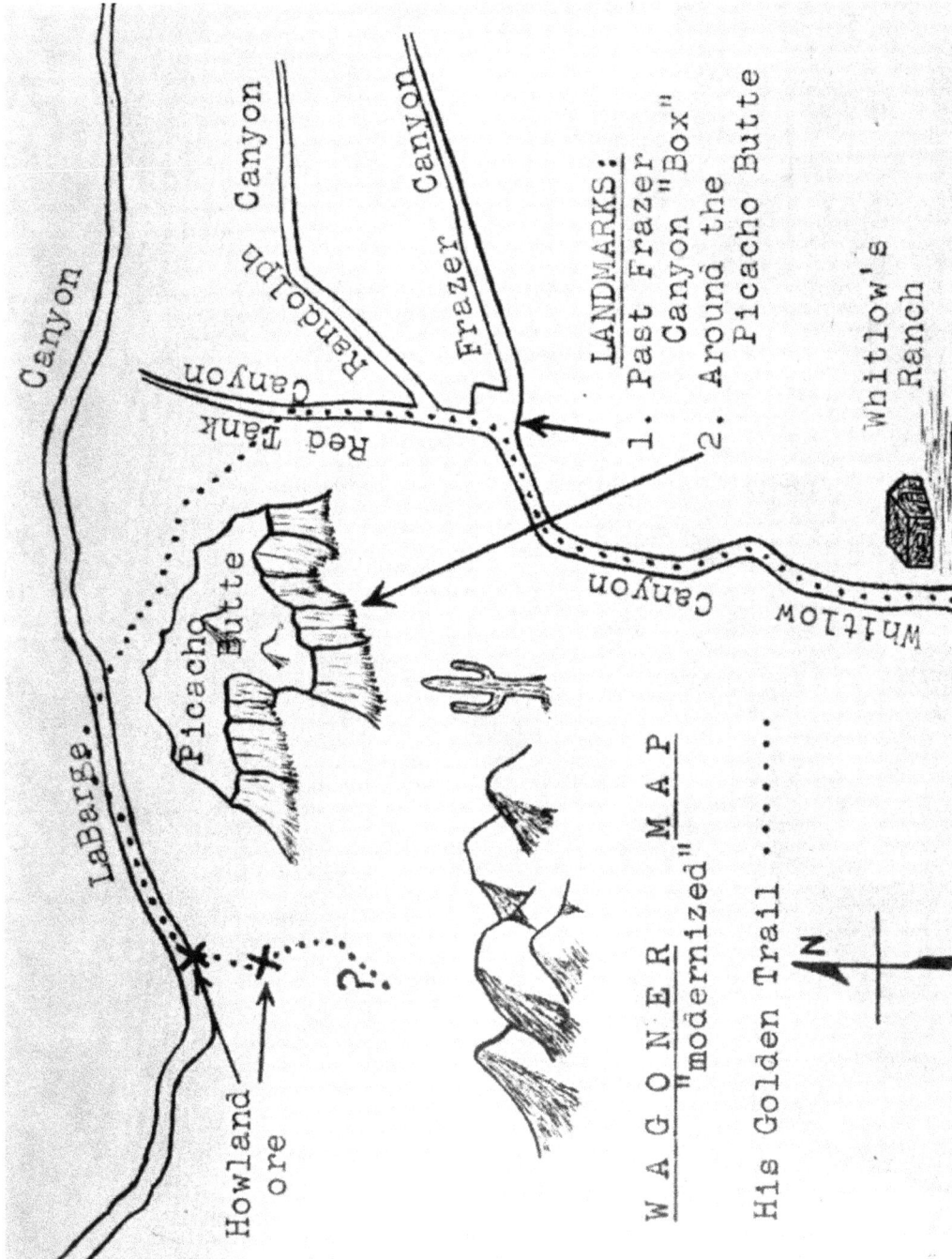

WAGONER MAP "modernized"

His Golden Trail ......

LANDMARKS:
1. Past Frazer Canyon "Box"
2. Around the Picacho Butte

Frazer Canyon

Randolph Canyon

Red Tank Canyon

Canyon

LaBarge

Picacho Butte

Howland ore

Whitlow Canyon

Whitlow's Ranch

N

Wagoner's mapped trail[24] to the ledge of rose quartz bonanza ore which he found in the Superstitions.

"Mines nearby (inset) on mapped trail!" say these Spanish miner's signs found on a cliff of the Peralta-mapped mountain near others. But will the map between, discovered by unlucky Ruth, again divulge their locations?[26]

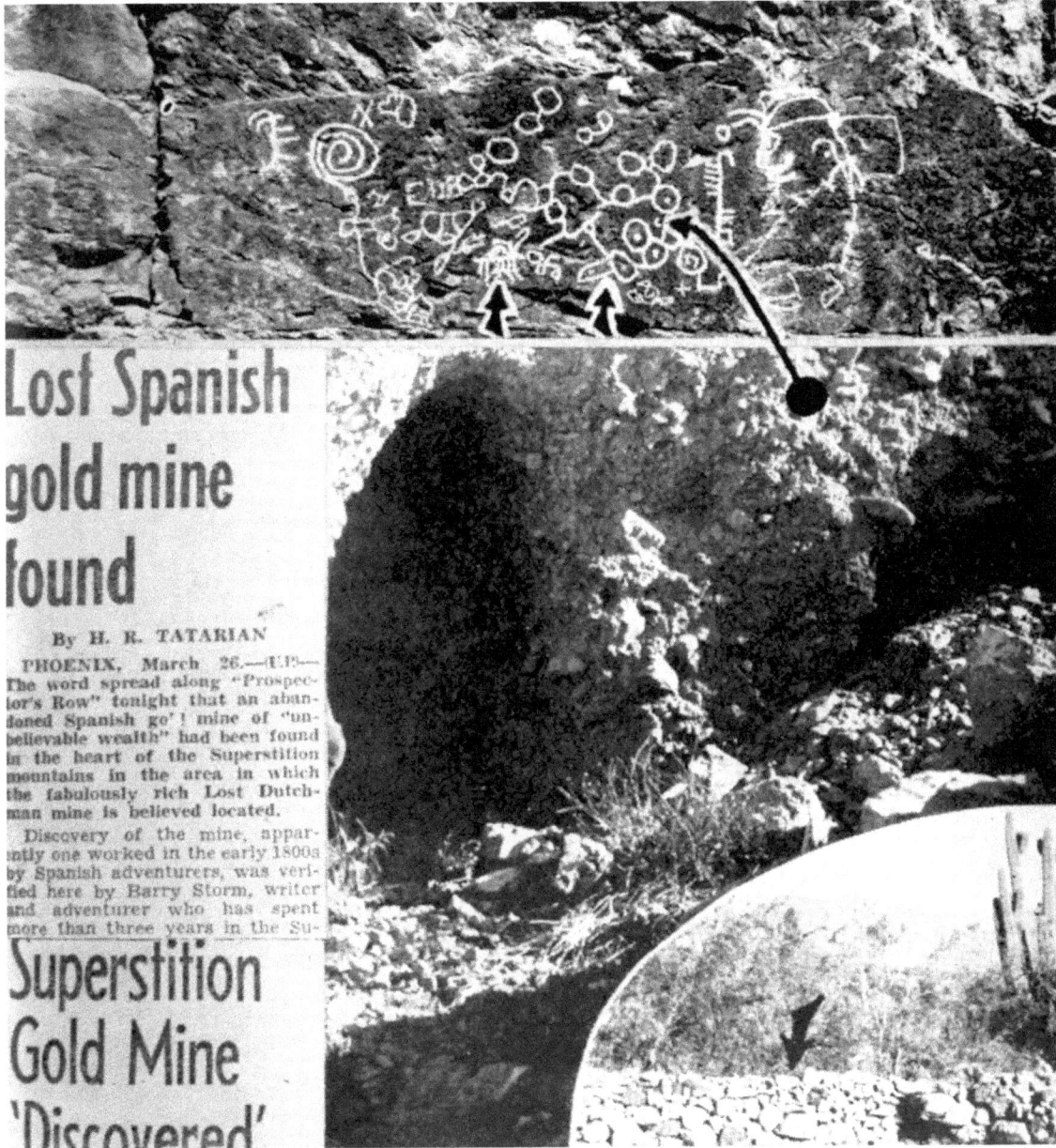

Within the image, newspaper clipping text:

Lost Spanish gold mine found

By H. R. TATARIAN

PHOENIX, March 26.—(UP)—The word spread along "Prospector's Row" tonight that an abandoned Spanish gold mine of "unbelievable wealth" had been found in the heart of the Superstition mountains in the area in which the fabulously rich Lost Dutchman mine is believed located.

Discovery of the mine, apparently one worked in the early 1800s by Spanish adventurers, was verified here by Barry Storm, writer and adventurer who has spent more than three years in the Su-

Superstition Gold Mine 'Discovered'

The Peralta master map[27] (top) indicated by other signs.[28] Note miner with candles in hat and ore sack on back **walking toward** involved region where (short arrows) Weaver's Needle (turn tip up) and Peralta-mapped mountain are recognizably shown. Tunnel sign (long arrow) located mine (below) in 1940[29] near (inset) breastworks built when massacre impended.

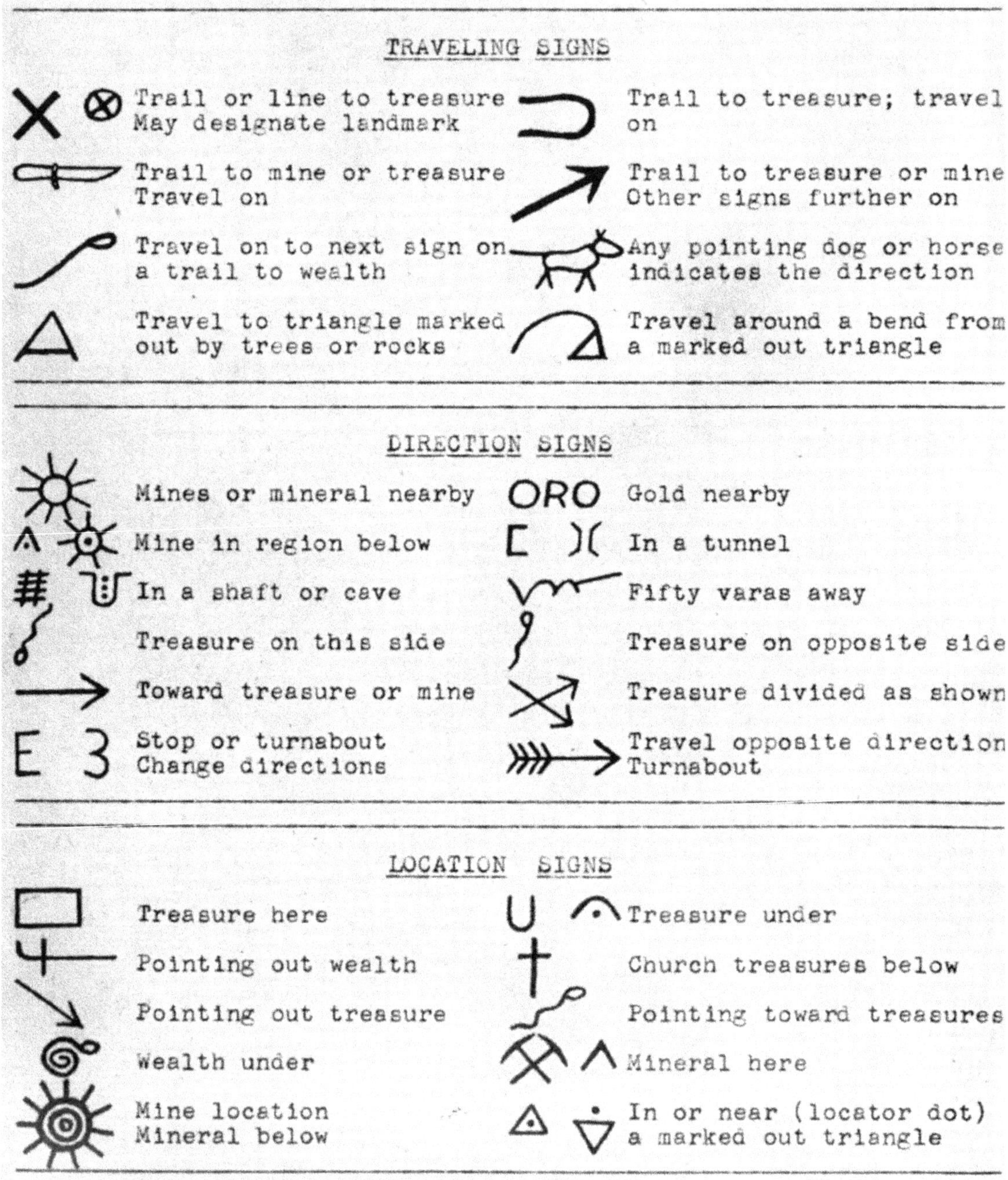

TRAVELING SIGNS

X ⊗	Trail or line to treasure May designate landmark	⊃	Trail to treasure; travel on
	Trail to mine or treasure Travel on	➚	Trail to treasure or mine Other signs further on
	Travel on to next sign on a trail to wealth		Any pointing dog or horse indicates the direction
△	Travel to triangle marked out by trees or rocks	△	Travel around a bend from a marked out triangle

---

DIRECTION SIGNS

☀	Mines or mineral nearby	ORO	Gold nearby
Λ ☀	Mine in region below	[ )(	In a tunnel
# ᵾ	In a shaft or cave	Vᶬ	Fifty varas away
⌇	Treasure on this side	⌇	Treasure on opposite side
→	Toward treasure or mine	⤬	Treasure divided as shown
E 3	Stop or turnabout Change directions	⇶→	Travel opposite direction Turnabout

---

LOCATION SIGNS

▭	Treasure here	U ⌒•	Treasure under
4	Pointing out wealth	✝	Church treasures below
↘	Pointing out treasure		Pointing toward treasures
◎	Wealth under	⚒ Λ	Mineral here
☼	Mine location Mineral below	△• ▽	In or near (locator dot) a marked out triangle

---

Signs[80] of Treasure!

3. SIGNS OF TREASURE

Signs of treasure,[30] those intriguing crosses and other singular marks which usually adorn lost mine or treasure maps or which are sometimes found cut into rocks and trees, were quite purposely meant to be enigmatical. And yet, even though the key to a proper interpretation may depend upon the **slant** of an arrow, for instance, the logic of creation and usage may be easily reasoned out.

Indeed, if the circumstances involved are considered such cabalistic symbols become startlingly similar though centuries in time and oceans of space separate individual uses. So the arrows used by wealthy Moors in Africa and Spain and by Spanish adventurers in America for indicating the way to hidden riches assume an identical meaning because they were used for an identical purpose.

Such an arrow when flying horizontal, for instance, could hardly mean anything but "travel on toward treasure." And when pointing down into the ground it must invariably be saying, "dig for the treasure here." But if unusual pains are taken with a normally plain and universally understood arrow in adding feathers or other decorations to the shaft **for a secret meaning,** and since the only other meaning which could logically be given a pointer is that of a reversal of direction, then the feathered shaft would be fairly screaming, "turnabout for you are now traveling **away** from treasure."

Sometimes these symbols are individually conceived like the frontiersman's sheath knife pointing out his hidden cache or the crossed picks locating the rich mineral vein over which a prospector has just stumbled. More often, simply because people are not more subtle, the signs used are of quite plain intent like the simple cross cut into anything handy to designate an important landmark or treasure trail, or the sun symbol with radiating rays which from time immemorial has always indicated mineral wealth to all peoples of of all climes.

This common significance is particularly true if the map depicting **signs** is of Spanish origin or if the symbols are found in territory over which Spanish-Mexicans once roamed. For it was the Spaniards who were there first—and most often had occasion to hide or abandon the fabulous treasures and bonanza mines which are legendary throughout the West! And even though native Indian signs like the many-ringed Aztec sunburst were adopted their likeness of creation and purpose has led to a marked similarity in all the symbols which have been found accompanying mineral wealth and the treasures derived from mining. For instance, such variants of the cross developed as that used by adventurers with a purposely longer arm pointing out a treasure trail and that used by priests with a longer arm pointing down to the burial site of church wealth or artifacts. Others simply piled up stones or blazed trees at the three corners of a triangle enclosing their mine or treasure while those who saw that the purpose of the triangle would be easily understood by anyone who chanced upon it made their triangle to one side of the actual site and indicated this variation by a locator dot showing the true relative positions of triangle and treasure.

In many cases these symbols are actual symbolical representations of things used and encountered and were therefore easily understood by others in **like circumstances** however ambiguous they may appear today. Thus, instead of actually using muleshoes the symbolical "U" was cut into a nearby rock with the toe pointing out the direction and no one could mistake that it meant to "travel on" or "dig here" according to whether horizontal or vertical. In a like manner the box, symbolizing the chest in which treasure would be normally buried, could only mean a marking of the actual treasure site. Again, when mines were abandoned because of Indian raids or other reasons not involving an exhaustion of ore, the universal sun symbol with a conspicuous dot or extra circle added to its center would obviously signify that "here is the mine" or "mineral wealth is below." And ladders or stairs as obviously add "in a tunnel or shaft nearby."

When such symbols are interpreted in the light of circumstances **at the time they were made** they are found to do one or both of two things. Most commonly they merely locate the involved vicinity so the original hider of mine or treasure, who is already acquainted with topography and location details, may easily trace his own way back by having his memory refreshed at the proper places. Less often, the symbols, **when read in proper sequence,** give exact instructions for relocating an actual site. But, as might be logically expected, there are often two conflicting sets of signs, only one of which gives the true location to insure that anyone who chanced upon the marked trail to fortune would find himself baffled without the map or other memoranda which the original maker had intended as the key.

Signs found upon the ground then often lead on from the maps which serve first to locate the proper region and then therein the true signs. Sometimes this was accomplished by triangulation from two or more prominent landmarks which are outlined upon the map in recognizable detail so that by traveling around the obviously dominant one until its general contours match those drawn and then towards it until **both** outlines match from the **same point,** the exact position is refound from which the map had been sketched. Then duplicates of the true signs shown upon the map will be found in approximately the same relative positions upon the ground. More often the locator map is merely a rough sketch of an outstanding landmark but the purpose and method of use is the same simply because no landmark will appear exactly as mapped except from the side mapped.

In the Spanish-explored Americas, which included most of the West, many **antigua** mines and hidden treasures have already been refound through the cabalistic symbols indicating their presence or exact location. Often the Spanish word for gold—**"ORO"**—had been plainly cut into a nearby rock and it could only mean that "gold is nearby." Often, too, snakes replaced directional arrows but for identical purposes so if one were found crawling head first down a tree it would obviously indicate that "treasure is here." If crawling up, it must be saying, "the treasure is on the opposite side," and if it were coiled it is plainly proclaiming, "here is the treasure, underneath!" Yet in spite of this obviousness many of the present owners of maps depicting such signs or the finders of signs on the ground have not always been able to capitalize upon them simply because the directions are not detailed enough for a stranger to properly follow them, the principle reason why even well-authenticated mines or treasures are not always located even though their existence within a very definite region is known beyond doubt.

Sometimes, too, a particularly important symbol is actually a shadow or projected light sign[31] which becomes visible only at the time and from an observation point known by those alone who had a legitimate reason for following the trail to wealth. Such phantom signs have been created by rocks piled up so the shadow cast was in the desired shape for a short while. Or smooth-surfaced rocks were placed to that the sun would cause a reflection of the sign onto a shadowed cliff face nearby. Less often a hole was cut or stones piled up on a ridgetop so the sun would shine through at the appointed time, projecting the sign like a spotlight beam upon a shadowed opposite surface. In all cases the sun's position is the controlling factor and so **both** the time and observation point must be known.

All of the thirty-odd symbols illustrated seem to reoccur to the minds of treasure hiders of no matter what race or clime with an astonishing standardization of basic design, and roughly divide into traveling signs, direction signs and location signs. Often several of each go to make up a sequence of exact instructions. Yet no matter where found such symbols invariably indicate the presence of nearby mineral wealth or hidden riches and if successfully interpreted and followed become truly signs of treasure!

PART II

BONANZA
HISTORY

"For them still
 Somewhere on the sunny hill,
 Or along the winding stream,
 Through the willows, flits a dream;
 Flits, but shows a smiling face,
 Flees, but with so quaint a grace,
 None can choose to stay at home,
 All must follow, all must roam."

—ROBERT LOUIS STEVENSON

Often billowing thunderheads break suddenly upon the high Superstitions (left) in livid lightning, cannonading thunder, torrential rains. Then awe-struck savages say that their thunder gods are angry.[32]

1. THE LOST PERALTA MINES

Apache thunder gods were there first in the wild Superstitions. There a thousand ages before white men had set a name to that incredibly twisted maze of sheer canyon-chasms and lofty, weather-sculptured crags which rise abruptly like a lost world set apart high over the vast Arizona desert.

The thunder gods are still there in the weird immensity of their domain. But now they guard yellow, glittering gold—gold cursed with the stain of Apache blood and marked by bleached Spanish bones, gold often found and then as often lost again! All manner of men have searched for that gold and the eight fabulous bonanzas in which it lies hidden, are searching still. And more frenziedly than ever, for one of those bonanzas was 'discovered' in 1940[3] from which, it is said, a small fortune in fantastically rich ore was immediately shipped to the smelter! And now new, exciting clues have narrowed down the golden treasure hunt where the ill-fated Peralta expedition from Mexico first mined.

The year was 1846 then in the swashbuckling days of living history. In the days, too, of vast, uncharted wilds—and, the Peralta brothers hoped, of quick fortune for the daring. For family silver mines in Chihuahua, after two generations of furnishing a living in the pleasant manner due Spanish noblemen, were at last on the verge of exhaustion. And their owner, **Don** Miguel Peralta,[14] had just returned home from a sanguine **entrada** to the headwaters of the **Rio Salado** with a perfect remedy.

"The river drains a virgin wilderness," he told his eager sons, "in which gold anywhere will give clue to itself as errosion-borne placer particles in the riverbed. Follow the river then until you find such placer gold, and trace it back to its source."

This was excellent prospecting advice anywhere. And it was exactly what Pedro, Ramon and Manuel Peralta were doing as they journeyed for endless weeks down the ever-growing Salt

River, followed the rushing waters through high, sheer-walled gorges and past boulder-choked rapids. Occasionally they panned for gold where tributary streams came into the river or where sandbars and riffled bedrock made a natural gold trap. And always they pressed relentlessly on toward a horizon as distant and vague as the purple sunset clouds. Then at last on a lucky day they rounded an abrupt bend in the river's shadowed chasm to find before them (at the present site of Mormon Flat) a veritable paradise in that country of sun-baked, rainbow-hued rock ; a small, verdant valley in the middle of which LaBarge Creek, as yet unnamed, tumbled down in miniature cascades from a range of ragged mountains on the south. From the wild, unmapped Superstitions!

So was history made. And so began legend!

For there at the junction of the stream and the river they fell to work with shovel and goldpan as they had a hundred times before. But this one time in the drainage of virgin, mineralized wilderness where reddish ryolite and black basalt cut through gray-brown tuffa, where creamy feldspar, white quartz and greenish serpentine rose to the surface, the results were as inevitable as they had been for generations up and down the length of the Spanish-explored Americas. And gold was there, a fabulous treasure trove of bright, yellow flakes, caught beneath the sands of the riverbed from a million years of rock-pulverizing errosion above!

By this time limited provisions had dwindled. And Pedro, who as eldest brother held command, decided to split up their forces in the interest of speed. So he left Ramon and Manuel to build **arrastres**[36] and work the placer gold at their new-found desert oasis and set out himself upon the golden backtrail to ore.

Higher, ever higher then, he climbed from LaBarge into Boulder Creek, on up the tributary Needle Canyon, and so unwittingly into the very heart of the Apache thunder gods' own sacred mountains. And there, two miles or so northerly of a

"Gold!" says **ORO** in Spanish, to which the northwest pointer of the key marker far below exactly points. Other treasure signs,[26] linking the fabulous past to the present in a most fantastic way, explain, "In a mine below fifty **varas** on the mapped treasure trail!"

towering, hat-shaped peak, which he called **La Sombrera,** the placer trail thinned out and he fell to prospecting for the source of the gold upon the river far below.

First he tried a steep tributary canyon (now known as Bluff Springs), followed its brush and boulder-choked course upwards to Bluff Springs Mountain where he left as proof of his presence narrow crosscuts[37] on several veins. Again, he tried further up Needle Canyon and left another crosscut[38] on a hillside. Then finally, high upon the slopes of a basalt-capped, black-topped mountain a mile and a half due north of **La Sombrera,** he came upon four rich outcrops of reddish, gold-bearing quartz.[39] Four bonanzas in the raw!

Exciting weeks fled then while the wheel of fortune spun crazily. But soon provisions were gone and his mules were staggering instead under hundreds of pounds of fabulous, gold-speckled rock ready to be crushed in the **arrastres.** And Pedro, after the fashion of miners who must leave bonanza ore behind, went down into Needle Canyon below the eastern slopes of the black-topped mountain and from the end of a rocky ridge he drew a triangulation locator map.[21]

This map showed the respective outlines of the dominant **La Sombrera** to the south up-canyon so the proper canyon could be again relocated by merely traveling around the hat-shaped peak until its shape matched that drawn, and also the topographic outlines of the fabulous mountain to the west so it could, too, be refound by merely going up the proper canyon until its shape also matched.

And then Pedro returned to the river to find his brothers impatiently awaiting him.

Indians, it seemed, were the trouble—and a burning itch that a golden fortune would bring to anyone. Nor did Pedro's tale of yet more gold change their minds.

"We already have enough," explained Ramon and Manuel. "And we have decided to enjoy it while we may. We will go far south of the **pueblo,** Tucson, where cattle flourish and establish a great **rancho.** For here each day more savages come to prowl about and harass us. Soon we might be overwhelmed. Then what of our gold?"

"We part then," Pedro said. "For I am returning home after help to work the mines that I have found. So let us divide all equally. And I will give each of you maps should you ever desire to return here."

And the two copies of Pedro's map which went south into Sonora with Ramon and Manuel were bright threads in the amazing skein of golden disaster which Apache thunder gods were even then weaving in sardonic mirth. For the towering crags and endless chasms of the Superstitions were their own ancient domain, sacred ground[32] to be guarded with life and honor by every savage who feared the livid lightning, crashing thunder and roaring floods which often swept down from that mountain fastness upon the surrounding desert.

Then back from Chihuahua City to those same sinister mountains came Pedro again in the winter of 1847-48 with sixty-eight men and 200 mules. Back to golden fortune—and savage death!

Indeed, the very nature of that incredibly rough country, the shadowed canyons with each its labyrinth maze of countless arroyos which twisted and turned through solid rock or opened out suddenly into unsuspected hidden valleys, the dense thickets of prickly pear and cholla, mesquite and catclaw, the sheer, multi-colored cliffs above on which spire-like crags clustered together and the less steep lower slopes honeycombed with countless caves or choked with huge boulders and tumbled rock slabs, all made stealthy cover through which silent Apaches came like furtive phantoms. And continually warriors kept the gold-hungry invaders under maddening surveilance, occasionally transfixed a luckless miner with stone-tipped arrows that appeared from nowhere.

But Pedro was not a frontiersman to recognize these ominous portends of impending disaster. He was a miner and the mad, driving urge to dig quick fortune from the ground, the romantic, reckless impulse to search for yet more gold caused him to ignore the silent warnings. And he divided his strength into a handful of workers at the **arrastres,**[36] mining and prospecting groups and crews of packers which were scattered for miles through the mountains.

Soon then two more potential bonanzas[39] were discovered upon the steep slopes of a hill which jutted into Needle Canyon from the western side, forming thereby a triple right angle turn and for a short distance the only south slope. And directly across from this hill, in a steep-climbing arroyo which ran up the canyon's eastern side under towering cliffs, still a third vein[39] of rich, gold-bearing quartz was found. Later, one more mine site about three-quarters of a mile east of **La Sombrera** and near the western slope of LaBarge Canyon was located. But this latter mine, which was rediscovered in 1940[3], was merely a conglomerate deposit of gold nuggets in cemented gravel and was soon worked out. So there began in the Superstitions in 1847 feverish activity such as the mountains had never before witnessed.

Permanent camps, of which there are still traces, were built in Needle, Bluff Springs and LaBarge Canyons and in one of the numerous unnamed arroyos at the base of **La Sombrera** a stone hut[42] was erected from which Pedro could direct the mining nearby. Nearby, too, charcoal pits[43] in which to re-temper drills were dug and fired, trees were felled and hewed into mine timbers and always the shafts were sunk deeper into the gold-quartz ore which busy muletrains hauled to the **arrastres** near the river for grinding.

By this time the winter of 1847-48 had fled, the brief desert spring had long since faded and the heat of summer was on the wane. And then suddenly the Apaches, who had been content with occasional raids upon isolated packers and miners, began to attack in earnest. Roving bands of warriors appeared—an advance guard to cover the massing together of hundreds of braves by wily Apache chieftans with which to destroy at one blow the invaders who so tenaciously worked and fought within their sacred mountains.

Pedro's first news of the impending catastrophe came from from the river on an unlucky September day with a packer who staggered into camp to gasp out with his life a horrible tale of massacre at the **arrastres.** For like an angry, frothing tidal wave the Apaches were sweeping inexorably over everything before them in superstitious frenzy, had slaughtered the astonished workers on the river, were even then ambushing guards and packers. Then other men rushed into camp to inform Pedro that death was indeed upon them, that fierce hordes of savages were swarming into the Superstitions in overwhelming numbers.

Pedro immediately ordered his mules burdened with foolish golden treasure. And while the miners fought a desperate rear-guard action, he buried the remaining bulk of it nearby, cutting in solid rock near his main camp in LaBarge canyon a master map[27] to its location and the locations of all his mines. And in Needle Canyon, upon the rocky point from which he had made his original locator map, he erected a hasty key marker[33] by driving stones into a giant saguaro cactus to point out his master map and nearby miner's signs so that the original locator map would serve as the real key to all. Then like chaff before a wind he fled with his band in frenzied haste toward the open desert on the west.

But he fled into a trap!

Apaches were there, were indeed everywhere—hideously painted savages riding madly upon bareback ponies, screaming, fighting, killing in a virtual blood-thirsty, religious frenzy. In uncounted hordes they drove the miners back against the solid mountain cliffs within sight and sound of the present ghosttown location of Goldfield. Then from all sides came a deadly hail of arrows, savagely-hurled lances . . .

The Apaches promptly scalped their victims and looted the packtrain, thinking that they thus had obtained a fortune in booty. But unwittingly they left a far greater fortune behind—yellow dirt, so they thought, which they distainfully dumped upon the ground.

Many decades later in 1914 two prospectors, C. H. Silverlock and a partner, digging in curiosity amid the debris of a massacre, found part of it there—$18,000 in glittering golden concentrates[44]!

But of the source of that gold and of the hiding place for possibly a million dollars more of the main bulk of it which unlucky Pedro Peralta buried from nearly a year's bonanza mining production the thunder gods alone knew the secret!

The Peralta-mapped mountain from across Needle Canyon above key marker[33] located at lower end of (dotted line) an ancient trail on which above (long arrow) a Spanish muleshoe[40] (inset) was found. Short arrows locate (top) Spanish miner's signs and (lower) the arroyo in which Adolph Ruth's remains[41] were discovered.

Weaver's Needle from pass between East Boulder and Needle Canyons, locating (arrow) hill of the horse's head which forms the only south slope where (below) The Dutchman's natural face,[51] Apache horse's head marker[46] and Spanish-style crosscut,[38] clue to nearby mining, were found.

2. HIDDEN APACHE GOLD

Now the invaders had indeed been destroyed to the last man. But there still remained in the sacred domain of the thunder gods the sacrilegious work that they had wrought. And these crude mine shafts and the golden ore would doubtless be found by other foreign men to bring an invading horde once more into the mountains that were god. Should this occur again, said the medicine men holding solemn council upon the matter, the Apaches might be forever cursed by storms and floods and all manner of the natural disasters which angry deities could contrive. So it was decreed that a band of thirty squaws and two youths would be sent back into the Superstitions to cover the mines and destroy all traces of the fabulous workings.

And there in the mountains this work party labored for one full moon, throwing ore and hastily abandoned tools back into the shafts. Then they covered the mines with stout logs which in turn were covered with the natural caliche cement that hardens into rock. And over the whole they placed in cunning Indian fashion yet another covering of dirt and surface stones to match the surrounding ground.

But with all this care the Apache squaws left one mine open because they thought it so well isolated and naturally hidden that it would never again be found. Yet it was the most fantastic bonanza of them all, a mere newly-started, shallow pit which was destined to become America's most sought for lost mine.

It was located, according to one of the Apache youths[45] who many years after told of his part in hiding Spanish bonanzas, in a steep-climbing arroyo high upon a mountainside where no white prospector would normally think of looking for gold. But gold was there in plenty, a bright yellow ribbon of it in a narrow vein of rose quartz. It lay under towering cliffs which overhung the whole arroyo, within plain sight of nearby Weaver's Needle.

Below was a secret marker[46] erected by the Apaches, an eight-foot high boulder hoisted upon the skyline of a ridge which, because it formed an abrupt bend in the north-south trending Needle Canyon, formed also for a few hundred yards the only south slope. This boulder had been chiseled to look like a rampant horse's head with mouth open, one ear laid back and with the other ear standing straight up. But it was only so recognizable against the sky when viewed from down canyon a short ways to the north. Upon this same hill, also, but to the west, were two more mines while still a third lay beyond the head of Needle Canyon and to the east of the hat-shaped peak there.

An enterprising mine hunter[47] heard the old Indian's story a couple of decades ago and offered him all the whiskey he could drink from then on if only he would take him into the mountains and point out the mines' locations. But though the Apache would readily enough give him directions, which of course proved useless to a stranger, he would not himself venture into the Superstitions for all the "firewater" in Arizona. The gold, he said, was cursed with Indian blood and death would be certain. Vengence of the gods did not fail.

Strangely, the story was verified many years previously in the 1870's by one of the older Indians of the tribe who was covertly keeping an eye upon things with the advent of roving cattlemen who occasionally worked their herds through the mountains. For in order to do this effectively the Apache thought it expedient to become friendly with Phil LaBarge and his partner, Charlebois, who were grazing a large herd of cattle dangerously close to the hidden mines at the time, and who since have left their names attached to two of the canyons in the Superstitions. And he often appeared at their camp, related Mart Charlebois[48] in 1938, son of the pioneer cattleman who then as a boy of fourteen rode with the herd.

One day LaBarge went hunting with the boy, climbed Bluff Springs Mountain, the Peralta-mapped, black-topped mountain and many of the lessor hills in between and around. Always together, the two of them covered much ground. And then a few days later when the hunt had been all but forgotten the old warrior appeared in camp again.

Casually he questioned LaBarge, asked him if he hadn't been out hunting upon that particular day. When LaBarge answered that he had, the Apache said that he had seen him with the boy at the time on top of a nearby hill, adding as casually but with solemn amusement: "Me see you stand on ninety million dollars!" And that no doubt was his untutored way of expressing untold mineral wealth in a form which white men could understand.

To LaBarge, who knew of the tales of nearby massacre and of lost Spanish mines, and who had seen with his own eyes upon several occasions samples of the course gold which The Dutchman was getting somewhere nearby even then, the implications were plain And he immediately pressed the aged Indian for details, learning finally by roundabout questioning that he had been seen from below Needle Canyon. This enabled him to narrow down the possible hilltops from which he would have been visible to the black-topped mountain and several nearby ridges. But it proved to be useless information for the mines had been well hidden indeed.

Just how well hidden the mines were—and still are—Abe L. Reid,[49] a pioneer cowboy and miner, found out in 1930 when he stumbled upon a solitary piece of bonanza gold ore upon northern slope of the black-topped mountain. Because he was "of the people and of the land" he immediately sought the help of "Old Jim," an aged Apache friend of many years standing who had, he knew, helped to hide Spanish mines nearby during the wild days of his youth. So the Indian (verifying in detail the story of his co-worker without knowing that he had spoken on the subject) explained to Reid, without divulging exact sites, that the workers of long ago had been split up, part of them hiding an upper group of mines and part of them a lower. And he had been the youth who had remained upon a black-topped hill due north of the sombrero-shaped Weaver's Needle to help hide four mines upon its slopes.

The deepest of these mines, he said, was fourteen of the Mexican ladders made by notching steps in logs—about seventy feet. And it was bell-shaped as it went down because of the way the ore had been crudely gouged from it[50]. But all four mines were so well covered by caliche-cemented logs that a packtrain could be driven over them without disclosing their locations.

Abe Reid readily enough recognized the Indian's black-topped hill as the same one on which he had found his piece of gold ore. And though he searched carefully there for two years he could not locate the hidden mines from which it must have come and decided finally to let the thunder gods keep their secret.

And the thunder gods have kept that secret very well indeed!

Abe L. Reid (inset closeup), pioneer Arizonian, whose burro-train took him into the Superstitions where he found a piece of bonanza Peralta ore[49] but not the hidden mines from which it must have come.

In the wild vastness of Western deserts there are other treasures than gold for those with eyes to see and soul to feel.

3. GOLDEN SKEIN

The Apaches had hidden the mines well indeed. But they had reckoned without Pedro's two brothers who had gone to Sonora! And there with the passing years Ramon and Manuel had not fared quite as well as they had anticipated.

Of course they had become gentleman ranchers with the golden fortune that they had brought from the Superstitions. But then, alas, they discovered after a time that there was some little difference between merely raising cattle and in selling them at a profit.

In spite of this decided lack of success in the grand manner to which they had been born Manuel was entirely content with their little kingdom. And he had married the daughter of a nearby rancher, Fernando Gonzales, and now had two children. But not so, Ramon!

Ramon had remained single and footloose. And to vary the staid life of which he had become a part he often rode to the nearby mining village of Cananea where he periodically drowned his boredom in a mad whirl of wine, women and song. There, too, in the **cantina** he found sort of a second-hand thrill in the convivial company of adventurers from all over the world.

This latter to Ramon was no small attraction for in his secret heart he often wished that he possessed like them the reckless hardiness to engage in a dangerous enterprise. And so he struck up a friendship with two of these adventurers, Jacobs, a German, and Ludi, a Hollander, who were together working a small nearby prospect. Before long they had become Ramon's inseparable companions, and with many tales to relate of a wide world over which they had roamed. But Ramon in return could only tell them of the bonanzas far to the north which his brother had found.

At these golden stories of course the two adventurers continually scoffed in a good-natured way. Bonanzas in that desolate wilderness? Well, perhaps. But if so, why was not Ramon even now up there adding to his wealth?

And so matters stood upon a day in June, 1860 when Ramon and Manuel received word of the death of their father, Miguel.

One of them, the sorrowful missive stated, would now have to return home to care for the estate—the old silver mines and the business properties in Chihuahua City and Monterrey where the elder Peralta had invested the gold that Pedro had brought him years before—since Pedro had never returned from his last adventure and must be accounted lost. So the two brothers decided between them that Ramon should make the trip, being then both free and willing. And thus it happened quite casually that Ramon set out upon the east-bound journey that took him for the last time to Cananea.

There in the little village he paused, before traveling on across the mountains, to bid his miner friends a last goodbye. Together the three went to the **cantina** and drank a toast to the future success of all. And then a thought occurred to one of the adventurers. What now of the fabulous mines of which Ramon had so often boasted? How was he going to keep his oft-repeated promise to prove that they really existed?

Indeed, Ramon stated, the matter was simplicity itself. And from his luggage he produced the map which Pedro had given him. It would, he said, show them exactly upon which one of the hills in the Superstitions near **La Sombrera** the mines[39] were located on, should they desire to go there. At any rate Pedro had never returned from his last adventure and the map was worthless to Ramon himself since another government[52] now held the land. But Ramon's friends might some day find it useful. If so, they were very welcome to the treasure which Ramon would never see.

And then he gave the two adventurers detailed directions for reaching the proper region from the south. From that direction of approach over the desert there, Ramon told them, they would have to go up the first deep canyon from the western end of the range, climb northward over the backbone of the mountains until they came within sight of a huge, **sombrero**-shaped peak, travel downward past the base of this **La Sombrera** into a long canyon running north until at last they found on the east side a tributary canyon which was very deep, pot-holed and densely wooded with scrub oak. Then they were to turn about and go back southward up this tributary canyon until they reached a point where the outlines of the hat-shaped peak to the south and of a black-topped mountain to the west both matched from the same place the outlines upon the map. From this spot they would then be looking upon the mapped mountain upon which Pedro had found four mines.

Jacobs and Ludi, it must be acknowledge, accepted both Ramon's instructions and his map with a grain of salt as it were. And yet, as they admitted then, they might possibly look into such an intriguing matter someday, if only for curiosity's sake.

Eleven years went by then during which both Ramon and his map were virtually forgotten. But finally the adventurers own mine played out, bringing with the necessity of seeking new fields memory of Ramon's golden tale. Probably there was no truth in it, reasoned Jacobs and Ludi. Yet what could they lose by finding out? And didn't Ramon's wealth lend considerable weight to the fascinating possibilities he had pointed out!

So at last in the spring of 1871 the two adventurers, more from curiosity than valid reason, treked northward from Mexico and on into the Superstitions. Then following the directions which one of them had jotted down upon the map, they finally reached the point in Needle Canyon from which it had been made to find amazingly that the map did indeed match both the high, hat-shaped peak and the black-topped mountain there. No doubt, too, they discovered in the region enough evidence of Pedro's presence to excite their enthusiasm. And they went doggedly from the site after site of now-hidden mines and hunted persistently over the nearby hills until at last they had stumbled upon the newly-opened, shallow bonanza-to-be which the Apaches had left uncovered twenty-three years before— glittering, golden rock which the Indians had thought would never again be found!

Ramon had been right after all. And small wonder that he was a rich man. For here was fabulous ore[53] of such dazzling wealth as to stagger the imagination, ore such as even they had never seen before in the richest of Mexican mining camps —beautiful rose quartz that was almost a third yellow metal!

But it had been found not alone by Jacobs and Ludi. Once again the bright thread of disaster was becoming entwined in the golden skein!

Once again from the vast Arizona desert Apache thunder gods were gathering for the kill.

GLOBE, Feb. 5—R. Petrasch 75, known as "Pete", shot and killed himself in the city bar, where he was a caretaker of ...h-Ba-Go-wah, Wednesday afternoon.

A note indicated he had killed himself because of failing eyesight.

He had gone to Justice of the Peace Clyde Shute last Monday and had a statement prepared. The statement said: "I am now 75. I was born in Germany May 21, 1867, and came to the United States when one year old. I am a citizen of the United States. In case of accident or death notify Herman Petrasch in Superior."

He had spent most of his life here. He prospected for many years and spent considerable time in looking for the Lost Dutchman mine.

Goldfield ghost town, once a bonanza mining camp,[54] near the western end of the Superstitions. Here The Dutchman and Wiser dug placer gold before finding their fabulous mine in the nearby mountains, here (inset clipping) Reinhart Petrasch[51] began his many searches. Below is the monument[55] erected at Apache Junction to The Dutchman and his world-famed lost mine.

4. WISER'S BONANZA

For some weeks now two other men who had outfitted in Florence, a frontier village some thirty-odd miles south of the still unmapped Superstitions, had been prospecting at the western edge of the mountains near the present location of Goldfield[54]. And both of these two Jacobs, Walz, "The Dutchman," and his partner, Wiser, were already well enough know in even that wild west as thorough-going scoundrels, capable of most anything.

Just where the two originally German immigrants had first met is not definitely known. Walz for a time worked in the early diggings of the famed Vulture Mine near Wickenburg before he was finally caught "highgrading" — stealing rich pieces of ore — and was fired. After that he seems to have drifted south to the Mexican border where he ran into Wiser, an itinerant carpenter whom no one would any longer trust with a job. And the two struck up a prospecting partnership together.

At the time, in fact, it was no particular secret that they had already struck "a rich spot of placer" gold[56] and had opened it up with a trench dug on the later-named Black Queen claim. But before prospecting further back in the Superstitions for the possible source of such gold, they had returned in the spring of 1871 to Florence to find someone who could build them two portable dry washers with which to more quickly work out the placer deposit. And they were directed to a local cabinet maker, another German now remembered only as "Frank," who made them the machines. Later, Frank[57], himself, recalled that while waiting for the dry washers The Dutchman had offered him a job and had speculated considerably upon the possibility of finding rich Spanish mines which Apaches were rumored to have hidden in the Superstitions. But Frank refused both the bait and the job because he knew nothing about mining. Perhaps, too, he felt that it was safer in town for the

Indians, still hostile, would be doubly dangerous to any white man caught in the sacred domain of their thunder gods.

So by one of those strange coincidences then which often happen in real life though they are too unbelievable for stories The Dutchman and Wiser worked out their placer gold and began prospecting the Superstitions at the same time that Jacobs and Ludi had just found their shallow bonanza. And working eastward, they pitched camp at last in Needle Canyon and started to cook an early supper. Then the faint, far-away sound of metallic pounding drifted down canyon to their astonished ears, the sound of steel upon rock. The unmistakeable hammering of miners!

Walz and Wiser turned to each other with eyes suddenly glittering. And in that instant each of them knew that the other was thinking exactly the same thing. Legendary mines! Spanish gold hidden by Indians! Wealth free for the quickest shot!

But was it fierce Apaches who had returned for gold to trade to foolish white men for guns with which to kill them? Or had another stumbled upon the legendary secret?

These, alas, were questions which needed only one answer! For if the odds were anywhere near even the two Germans had little to fear. Both were deadly shots, armed with the best guns of thir day, and the element of surprise would be in their favor. So Wiser grabbed up his .45-70 Springfield musket and Walz his .45-90 Sharpes. And then toward the sound of the pounding they went with stealthy softness, up Needle Canyon beyond the black-topped mountain which Pedro had mapped, and toward Weaver's Needle. And as the pounding grew louder, they suddenly spied Jacobs and Ludi working in a shallow pit high upon an eastern hillside. Working in a mine!

This opportunity for fortune neither Walz nor Wiser[23] could resist. From ambush they levelled their rifles. Then the crashing thunder of gunfire shattered the mountain silence, echoed and re-echoed in fading crescendo . . .

Early the next morning Wiser and The Dutchman were on their way to dispose of the bodies of their victims and examine the mine that fate had placed in their hands. And they went up Needle Canyon with mounting excitement, climbed the steep arroyo to the mine, then halted there in amazement. For the bodies of the two they had shot had apparently vanished into thin air!

But they had disappeared only from the murderous Germans.

Jacobs and Ludi, both mortally wounded, had fled unseen in the night for the low pass at the head of Needle Canyon that would let them out of the mountains on the south. Ludi died enroute. But Jacobs, stumbling on alone, finally reached Andy Starr's[53] cabin on the desert beyond. And there he collapsed in Starr's arms, babbling wildly about Spanish-mapped mines and hidden ambushers before he, too . . . died!

Meanwhile, back in the mountains, Walz and Wiser were examining the mine in a veritable frenzy of excitement. For fantastic ore was there to conjure forth roseate visions of unlimited wealth, a reddish quartz vein that was almost a third solid yellow gold. And it was theirs, every glittering bit of it!

But, thought The Dutchman, wouldn't that ill-gotten wealth be worth just twice as much to one of them alone? Then the treacherous roar of his gun suddenly drowned the thunder gods raucous laughter.

Deaf to Wiser's stricken screams then Walz cooly left him to die in the mine that he had murdered to obtain. And he returned to camp, methodically gathered up all of his partner's possessions—his dutch oven, fry pans, little coffee mill, even the bag of assorted nails that Wiser had always carried for his occasional carpentry work—and hid[58] them all under a nearby boulder in Needle Canyon, thus concealing forever, he thought, the evidence of his treachery.

In the meantime Wiser fled as had the two he had helped to kill. And friendly Pima Indians finally found him wandering in delirium on the desert beyond and carried him to the nearest white man's habitation, Colonel J. D. Walker's ranch near Florence. There for days Wiser hovered between life and death, telling his incredible story of murder, bonanza gold and greedy treachery a little at a time.

By way of proof he made Jack Walker a crude map[23] showing a way back to the mine somewhere northeast of Weaver's Needle. But the Walkers, growing rich even then from the Veckol Mine which Pima Indians had showed them, and doubtless knowing full well the unsavory reputation of the two Germans, were either not well enough impressed by the chance for more wealth in the Superstitions to risk Apache death for it or were more probably too wise to be taken in by Wiser's obvious attempts to gain revenge upon The Dutchman.

And so in Walker's home Wiser died as he deserved, himself a victim of the thunder gods' curse which he had invoked.

Portrait of a burro, the prospector's loyal companion, whose shod hoofs many generations later often leave tell-tale streaks of oxidizing iron on rocks to indicate ancient trails.

Western cliffs of the Superstitions near Goldfield from which The Dutchman watched his backtrail toward Phoenix on the way to his fabulous now lost mine beyond the (inset) first natural face located two miles east toward the wild interior of the mountains. Barry Storm is in foreground.

5. LOST DUTCHMAN MINE

The Dutchman, by this time back in the Superstitions, had gathered up his first sack of fabulous ore. Soon he appeared in Florence[57] with it where word of his strike spread like wildfire. And there for days he squandered his gold in an uproarious manner and regaled everyone who would listen with expansive tales of his new-found bonanza. It was an old Spanish workings, he repeatedly said. But of its location—ah, that was the secret worth a king's ransome!

It was inevitable then that the more baffled and envious people of Florence began asking about Wiser's whereabouts and talking much of the conspicuousness of his absence. For hadn't he gone into the Superstitions with The Dutchman? And wasn't he entitled by the prospector's unwritten code to half of the freely spent gold?

Dark rumors were these, intimating darker treachery and worse. And like all rumors founded in envy and suddenly aroused greed they grew overnight almost to ugly proportions. Then Walz publicly and foolishly replied to them with a hair-raising tale of an Indian attack in which Wiser and been killed. So the cat sprang out of the bag!

And Walker, out upon his nearby ranch, hearing of this dramatic proof for the tale that Wiser had told him, wisely decided to say nothing at all of either Wiser's burial there or of the map which Wiser had made. For someday he might, himself, wish to look into the source of all this wealth, and he probably would have was not the Veckol Mine even then making him a rich man.

So Walz vanished from Florence as abruptly as he had appeared. And then weeks later he turned up again with more of his fantastic ore, but this time in Phoenix where no one knew about Wiser. There he again went on a drunken spree, told even wilder tales than before of his bonanza—and promptly whipped the little village into such a state of high excitement that practically every able-bodied man there made immediate and secret preparations to follow him. But Walz was no fool, drunk or sober. And he vanished suddenly one night, dragging a blanket behind his burros to wipe out his trail.

Breathless weeks followed while scores of would-be trackers awaited The Dutchman's return. Then suddenly he was there in their midst like a wraith from the desert, this time with a burro-load of hand-picked ore which he sold to Goldman and Company's store, adding to the frenzy of pop-eyed watchers. For hasty calculations, based upon the weight capacity of his burro, proved this ore to be worth more than $10,000 a ton!

And this time, after his usual spree, The Dutchman upon leaving town not only found a stampede-sized crowd waiting to follow but saw that many more were already camped out upon the desert, thus hoping to intercept him.

After that he continually changed his course, usually entering the Superstitions from the western end as he had upon his first prospecting trip so that he could watch his backtrail for miles into the desert. Then when a particularly zealous follower did come close he would head for the rough, wild region around Weaver's Needle where he would vanish without a trace or lead his trailer upon a deliberate wild goose chase, sometimes swinging through the mountains only to come out again at Tortilla Flat or Tonto Basin.

On one of these occasions he appeared one evening at Blevins'[60] cabin near the present site of Roosevelt while Blevins was off on a trip to Globe. And Blevins' son put The Dutchman up for the night. When Blevins, himself, returned home the next morning and found that Walz had just left scarcely an hour before, after telling the boy that he was on the way to his mine, he grabbed up his rifle and took out upon the still-warm trail. But after a hard day's work he succeeded only in following the tracks to a little flat just south of the junction of

Reevis and Pine Creks. There The Dutchman must have discovered that he was being followed and started wiping out his trail as he went. For Blevins found the tracks ending as abruptly as though Walz had sprouted wings and flown off.

But Walz had in fact returned to his mine. And shortly afterwards he appeared in Tucson with two burro-loads of ore which he sold to Charlie Myers, an ore-buyer, for $1,600. George McClarty[61], Chuck Brown and one of the Poston brothers witnessed this sale. Then realizing from The Dutchman's conversation that he had never legally recorded a mining claim upon his location, they decided to follow him back to the mine and stake it for themselves. They followed him easily enough to the vicinity of Whitlow's Ranch on Queen Creek—and promptly lost the trail when Walz plunged into the twisting maze of steep canyons beyond.

Then, as though to mock their efforts, Walz returned again to Tucson almost immediately with a sackful of specimen ore samples which he had A. L. Pellegrin[62], an assayer, clean for him. Indeed, these pieces were so fantastically rich that Pellegrin, instead of charging The Dutchman for the job, accepted a chunk of the gold-engraved quartz which he later had cut into beautiful ring settings for his children.

On another occasion, Charles M. Clark[59] of Mormon Flat, at whose cabin The Dutchman sometimes stopped, tried to follow him and after a strenuous tour of the mountains found himself back hiding behind a mesquite tree at the Tortilla Flat spring while Walz sat down upon a rock and took it easy. After a time, and without even turning around, he calmly called to Clark to come out of hiding. Walz said that he had known Clark was following him all the time—and that he would kill him if he ever tried it again!

By this time everyone in Arizona Territory was thoroughly convinced that The Dutchman was secretly working a hidden bonanza. In fact, there could have been no doubt of it in the

face of his well-witnessed ore sales and continuous production
of the same type of fabulous ore for more than six years.   Yet
he seemed satisfied with merely bringing out enough of his
bonanza ore at one time to "have him a spree."   Perhaps he
also had a secret cache somewhere in the Superstitions where
he was accumulating a fantastic fortune against a time of need.
More than once Walz, himself[63], hinted at such a possibility.
And anyway the small frontier villages hardly offered opportunity for undue extravagance.

For years then this game of hide and seek continued with
Walz always proving to be the more canny outdoorsman.   But
in 1877 advancing age — Walz was now sixty-nine — and the
ever increasing persistence of followers as his golden fame
spread decided him to abandon his bonanza and retire.   And
he rented a plot of ground and an adobe hut, located near the
present intersection of Henshaw Road and Sixteenth Street
in Phoenix, from the pioneer Henshaw family[64] and settled down
at last to a life of ease and the prosaic pastime of raising chick-
ens and wine grapes.   There he guarded his secret with all the
delighted perversity of a child who knows something but won't
quite tell it.

In this little riverside community at the same there was by
one of those strange coincidences which sometimes occur a Ger-
man-speaking woman, an unusually light-skinned quadroon,
Julia Thomas, whose mother had been a servant in a German
family. And Julia, who owned an ice-cream parlor across from
the old City Hall, had a way with men and certain physical at-
tractions. Soon, people noticed, she was talking to The Dutchman in his native tongue, and he often—much too often, it was
said—took gifts of eggs and wine over to her home.   The wine,
people knew, was a very potent product of The Dutchman's
own skill.   And it was no secret either that soon he had given
Julia enough raw gold to buy a new fountain for her ice-cream
parlor.   All of which may have been reasons enough for the
strange friendship which developed.

In Phoenix, too, during this period, but "up-town," "Old Man" Petrasch, another German who had recently blown in from Montana with his two sons, Reinhart[51] and Herman, was busy establishing a bakery business. And The Dutchman could hardly fail to patronize a fellow countryman. To one of the Petrasch boys in particular, Reinhart, who made deliveries through his section of town from baskets slung on a yoke over his shoulder, Walz became very attached, probably because boy-like Reinhart often forgot his deliveries while he sat by the hour and listened to The Dutchman's fabulous tales. Once, when Reinhart confided to him that the bakery was about to go broke, old Walz gave the boy $500[51] in gold with which to buy equipment and a delivery wagon for himself.

Again, a year or so later, when Julia[65] needed some money one day to keep her wandering husband from coming home to roost, Walz told her to dig in his yard in a certain spot. She did, and brought up a tin can containing around $1,400 in gold dust and nuggets which she sold to Goldman's store. So the easy years rolled on. And then on May 3rd, 1887, just ten years after The Dutchman had last seen his mine, an earthquake[66] shook central Arizona, spending its fury along the fault which underlies the Superstitions near Phoenix and the Santa Catalinas near Tucson.

Old Walz, growing ever more feeble with the passing years, could not have known that this shock rolled boulders off of his mountain hillsides, caused cliffs to tumble and probably changed many of the landmarks which he had known. Anyway, it was so difficult for him to get around now that he had not thought about ever returning to his mine. But shrewd Julia had been nursing ideas of her own!

One day during the winter of 1891 she put it up to him, pointing out that he was now eighty-three years old. Soon, she said, he would be too feeble to go anywhere or he might even die. Then what of his long-boasted-about mine. Besides, his gold was admittedly running out and he wouldn't want to be caught penniless in his old age. So arguing thus she finally extracted his promise to take her into the Superstitions with the first fair weather of spring.

But fate once more intervened — or perhaps it was the thunder gods! And down from those same mountains and the vast wilderness beyond came flood waters suddenly rising until on February 19, 1891 the flood[87] which engulfed most of Phoenix also swept over The Dutchman's little hut. And he had to take shelter that evening in a cottonwood tree. There, after a night of exposure which brought on an immediate attack of pneumonia, Reinhart[51] found him the next morning and carried him upon his back to Julia's house.

Feeble with age, sick and homeless now, The Dutchman found his last sanctuary with Julia Thomas and Reinhart Petrasch who would not leave him. And realizing that death was at last upon him, Walz told his two friends the story of his mine. The shaft, he said, went down upon an eighteen inch vein of rose quartz which was studded with pinhead nuggets of gold with, beside it, a three inch hanging wall of hematite quartz that was itself about a third pure gold. Then as clues to its location he told them of a roofless, two-room house which he had made of heaped-up stones in the mouth of a large cave. The cave was near the bottom of a high bluff and faced northward for he had always kept a tarpaulin hanging in the entrance to keep out the north wind and rain[63].

After they had found this cave, which explained his ability to vanish from pursuers so easily, they were to go about a mile further up the same canyon, which trended north-south, until they found a ridge upon the end of which was a natural stone face[46] looking upward to the east. Directly across from this face, high in a narrow ravine, they would find the inclined entrance to his mine. The right canyon, he added, could be identified further by the tumbled ruins of an old Spanish-built stone house[42] near its head. Then he made a rough sketch map, starting from a first natural stone face[68] near the western end of the mountains, and sealed it in an envelope for Julia. And he died in her home on February 22, 1891[67].

Julia Thomas, the elder Petrasch and Herman that summer formed a partnership to search for the mine, financed by sale of the ice-cream parlor, while Reinhart[51] stayed behind to keep the bakery going. The three spent several months in vain searching, identified Walz's placer workings near Goldfield but never the location of his bonanza in the mountains beyond. And The Dutchman's crude map remained entirely undecipherable.

In later years, after old Petrasch and Julia had died and Reinhart had sold the bakery, both he and Herman searched together and then alone at various times. But both boys had paid little attention to Walz's statements during the years and found that they had jumbled or forgotten directions. In fact, Reinhart had forgotten even those verbal clues[63], which gathered together from the many different people who had heard them, localize by amazingly accurate descriptions the region in which verifying evidence of Walz's presence was later found.

On one occasion Walz had said, "You'll never find it, but **if you pass three red hills you have gone too far.**" Too far to the north he must have meant for the only three red hills are a bare half mile north of the Bluff Springs and Needle Canyons junction. Again, he once said that he could not be seen from **the military trail in the canyon below**, but that he could easily **watch the trail from his mine.** And then once more he told about having to climb a short ways from a steep ravine in order to **see Weaver's Needle to the southward from above his mine.** The shaft there must have faced west because he was particularly fond of detailing just how the **setting sun would shine through a break in the mountains** and glitter upon the ore.

Perhaps that ore still glitters there in iridescent splendor. For though a dozen lives and many fortunes have been spent in the search America's most famed lost mine—is still lost!

LaBarge Canyon (upper) which Dr. Thorpe first identified as the way to his gold, and (below) the Four Peaks on the opposite side of the Sal River over which he also searched.

6. DR. THORNE'S GOLD

One of the most deceptive of all things probably is the past. For just when one has decided that something may be called a definite historical fact, it often slides from under that convenient label to become a legendary mixture of truth and exaggeration which can be proven neither wholly true nor entirely false. And while this is really the actual status of Dr. Thorne's gold, the well-witnessed fact remains that he did once return from the Superstitions with a modest fortune in bonanza ore and then aroused the interest of the whole countryside in trying to find its source.

This all occurred in the late seventies,[69] perhaps in 1876 if a concensus of local memory can be trusted, though the date is not half so important as the gold. And Dr. Thorne, an enlisted member of the United States Army Medical Corps at the time, was stationed at Fort McDowel, some twenty-two miles as the crow flies northwest of Weaver's Needle. At the time, too, Fort McDowel was not only a frontier Army Post but the headquarters for an Indian reservation. So Dr. Thorne was engaged as much in looking after the physical welfare of the Army's Indian charges as of that of the soldiers.

In the squalor of the nearby Indian village then it was only natural that savages unaccustomed to confinement should fall ill occasionally of the most trivial ailments. And it was this fact, as Dr. Thorne himself later related, which led to his good—and then bad—fortune. For one day the Indian medicine man came after him in haste, having just failed himself to cure the chief's wife of a painful attack of indigestion.

In fact, Dr. Thorne found upon his arrival at the chief's tepee that the squaw's pain was so great and the medicine man's failure so obvious the Indians were already preparing for her sudden and untimely death. And suspecting from much experience that it was all caused by a gluttonous over-indulgence in the ration of white man's food which the Army furnished weekly, he went to work with his own medicines and promptly effected a cure that seemed nothing short of miraculous.

In that one village at least then Dr. Thorne suddenly found himself acclaimed as a public hero. And he was immediately asked to attend the council called by the chief to determine a suitable method of rewarding him. For wasn't one Indian life well enough worth anything that lay within their power to bestow? Then what did the white medicine man most desire? Could it be a young and handsome squaw? Or perhaps a swift horse? Or might it be yellow metal with which to purchase the pleasures of his own race? And the Indians did know[70] where much gold could be gathered in the mountains across the river!

Presented with such an alluring choice, Dr. Thorne of course made the inevitable decision. And so early the next morning he found himself riding with a party of braves who left the Indian village at Fort McDowell, rode due southeast toward Weaver's Needle which could occasionally be glimpsed in the distance and crossed the Salt River near the Mormon Flat ford to continue past many of the canyons which led down from the Superstitions. Then the Indians called a halt and told Dr. Thorne that he would have to be blindfolded the rest of the way so that he could not later return himself or lead other white men to the gold that was to be shown him.

Dr. Thorne readily enough consented to this condition even as he was busy taking a good all-around look at the canyon entrance, thinking, as he later confessed, that he had those high cliffs and the topography of the surrounding ground so well photographed in his mind that he would have no trouble in returning later. And then the party started up again while Dr. Thorne, blindfolded this time, concentrated his entire attention upon two clues—the laboring movements of his horse which indicated that they were climbing steadily higher into the mountains up a rocky-bottomed canyon, and a mental reckoning of the approximately three hours that the ride lasted. Then at last the Indians halted once more and told Dr. Thorne that he could now remove his blindfold.

Free to see again, Dr. Thorne found that they had stopped in a long north-south trending canyon, the eastern wall of which was formed at that point by the high cliffs of an equally long mountain. And from the canyon bottom where the horses were left he could just barely see the tip of a sombrero-shaped peak which he thought at the time looked like Weaver's Needle to the southward. Then the Indians led him up a steep tributary arroyo which seemed to run right into the shadows of overhanging cliffs, but instead ended finally in a miniature hidden valley. There Dr. Thorne saw, to his unbounded delight, a narrow, trench-like workings along a vein—and scattered profusely about countless pieces of quartz that were literally studded with yellow metal! There, too, much to the covert amusement of the Indians and to his own later chagrin, he immediately became so engrossed in sorting out the richest looking pieces of ore that he gained only the haziest impression of his surroundings.

Indeed, Dr. Thorne lost no time at all in gathering up every bit of the gold-speckled rock that he could carry. And he filled the saddlebags which he had brought along, stuffed all of his pockets until they threatened to burst and even took off his hat which he crammed full. Then when the Indians saw that he had nothing left in which to carry away more of the rock, they took him back to the horses, blindfolded him once more and led him back for the last time to the crossing upon the Salt River. And there they left him to ride on alone into Fort McDowel with his fortune, where he sold his golden rock for a reported $28,000 to the Army quartermaster.[69]

For the next few weeks Dr. Thorne, by his own admission, wandered around in a delicious roseate haze, telling all who would listen about his singular good luck. Then when at last the novelty of being a rich man had worn off somewhat, his thoughts turned to a way to become richer still by returning to the source of his gold. But, like so many others before and since, he soon discovered that for every landmark which he had observed there were a thousand counterparts and near duplicates.

In the years that followed then he attempted time after time to reconstruct the way he had gone blindfolded, to back trail himself to fortune. Once he tentatively identified the canyon mouth from which he had started as LaBarge Creek. Then thinking perhaps that the Indians had purposely started in one direction and afterwards had turned about to go another while he had been blindfolded, he scoured the Four Peaks country on the opposite side of the river. But always the more he searched the more confused he became. And at long last he succeeded only in spending the fortune which had been given him in a vain search for its source.

Once again thunder gods gold had become secret gold!

7. SOLDIERS' LOST VEIN

During the early 1870's, due southeast of the Superstitions and near General Stoneman's new military camp at Picket Post, was the start of one of the military trails which were being built by soldiers to facilitate pursuit of still-raiding Apaches into the mountain fastness beyond. And a habitual straggler, named Sullivan, was one of the working soldiers.

On a winter day then Sullivan sat down to rest awhile on the way back from work and idly picked up a handful of stones, among which was a particularly heavy, shiny black rock. Sullivan juggled it up and down in his hand for a long time and then as absently noticed that it seemed much softer than rock should be. So he broke a chip off and tried pounding it with another rock. When he saw that it was malleable he concluded that it must be lead sulphide. But in reality it was silver sulphide ore of bonanza richness!

Sullivan kept the piece that he had found though for some perverse reason he said nothing about it until after his enlistment had expired a short time later. Then he went to work on Charles G. Mason's ranch upon the nearby Gila River, often displaying his rock there but still not telling where he had found it. So when it became apparent that Sullivan never intended to prospect after his "lead" and drifted on elsewhere one day, Mason, himself, started to organize prospecting parties among his neighboring ranchers. And at last, on March 22, 1875, they found and staked out the future location of the fabulous Silver King Mine.

The strike itself was a major frontier sensation, and subsequent mining turned up one sensation after another—lenses of black silver sulphide running up to $20,000 a ton in richness. In fact, between 1875 and 1877—when Mason[71] sold out his interest—he and his partners shared in over a million dollars of production from a mere prospect. And then the Silver King Mining Company, incorporated May 5, 1877, stirred widespread talk of new, as equally fantastic returns from the development of a real mine—talk that was backed up in the next few years by another production record of three million dollars and the growth of Picket Post into the town of Pinal. But talk that caused Sullivan ironically to be responsible for another lost vein though his own had been found.

During this same period then, but while Mason was still part owner and superintendent of the Silver King Mine, two other soldiers—French-Canadian adventurers whose right names are either buried now in the archives of the War Department or were more probably never known—were just finishing a hitch in the Army at Fort McDowel. And news of the Silver King strike inclined them to seek work there for no other purpose than in merely seeing what a mining boom was like. So, when their enlistment had expired in the latter part of 1875, they decided to follow the military trail through the Superstitions in preference to a longer roundabout trip over the desert. And hiking due southeast from Mormon Flat they entered the mountains between Kayhatin and LaBarge Creeks, followed the trail past the prehistoric Indian ruins now known as Garden Valley over Black Mesa to West Boulder Canyon near its mouth, crossed the low ridge there that separates East and West Boulder Canyons, and went on up East Boulder Canyon along the west side of the Peralta-mapped mountain and toward Weaver's Needle which now was in plain sight, finally turning east on the trail to go through the low pass which separates East Boulder and Needle Canyons a scant mile apart. There, somewhere in the region between canyons, they flushed a deer accidently, fired at it at least once with their Army-issued .52 caliber Spencer[72] repeaters, and in the resulting chase came upon a partly exposed "reddish vein about a foot thick, halfway up a black-topped hill," to quote their own exact description.

But the two ex-soldiers did not know that it was fabulous golden ore which they had found. And they only knocked off a few pieces of the "pretty rock" for souvenirs—which they still had with them when they applied for work to Jack Frazer,[73]

the mining foreman of the Silver King at the time. They showed
Frazer their rock then, and were immediately hired. But Frazer,
after one astounded look, as immediately sent for Mason.

Mason of course arrived to confirm what Frazer was already telling the two ex-soldiers—that they had struck it rich!
In fact, from the few pieces which they had carried as relics was
recovered and weighed up right then over $500 in gold which
Mason placed to their credit upon the mine commissary books.
Then Mason, fresh in memory doubtless of the one bonanza
which he had gotten through an ex-soldier, approached the two
with the idea of forming a partnership for a share in their discovery.

He would outfit them, he said, from the commissary if they
would return to the Superstitions immediately and there stake
out a mining claim upon their golden ore. In the meantime, since
neither was a United States citizen, he would personally vouch
for them and so obtain the naturalization papers that would
make their claim valid. So agreeing to this arrangement the two
soldiers set out to backtrail themselves to fortune.

But riding behind with a rifle across his saddlehorn was a
peg-legged gambler named Smith who, it was later remembered,
left the mining camp at the same time! And the two ex-soldiers
were never seen again aliye.

Two weeks later both of their bodies were finally discovered by a coroner's posse in the present Quarter-Circle-U
Ranch range on the southern slopes of the Superstitions, where
they were buried after being identified by the Silver King marks
upon the equipment they had gotten from the commissary. Both
had been shot from ambush. And local opinion placed the blame
upon Smith though no formal charges were filed.

Many years afterwards, Smith who had vanished from Arizona only to turn up in Alaska almost immediately a wealthy
man, wrote to several former Arizona friends[74] from Alaska in

an effort to persuade one of them to go into the Superstitions and stake out there for a half interest a mining claim on bonanza gold ore to which he would furnish exact directions. But no one took his offer of fortune by mail seriously and he appeared afraid to return himself to the scene of a crime which might crystalize with his presence from suspicion to actual charges of murder.

Years later, also, one of the members of the coroner's posse, named Forest, who had helped to trail, find and bury the ex-soldiers when they failed to return to the Silver King Mine, said that at the time he had actually followed their tracks up into the second canyon east of Weaver's Needle in the Superstitions. He said that apparently the unlucky men were either heading toward Needle Canyon or had been there already and were fleeing when Smith had appeared. For most certainly the murderous gambler would have waited until they had disclosed the location of their fabulous vein since he could have easily afterwards overtaken them on horseback to keep that location secret forever.

Again, a short time later, a Superior miner named Phipps, said that he had successfully backtracked the two ex-soldiers to the source of their. bonanza ore. And when he returned to town greatly excited, he added: "It's less than two miles from Weaver's Needle toward the river. I seen a cool million dollars in sight!" But Phipps never lived to enjoy it. When he went down into his own shaft near Superior after tools with which to open up his new-found bonanza, an unexplained cave-in killed him.

So do the thunder gods guard their fatal treasure!

In 1875 the ex-soldiers, following a (lower arrow) military trail up East Bounder Canyon within plain sight of Weaver's Needle, turned east through the (top arrow) pass toward Needle Canyon beyond, jumping a deer where Barry Storm found their (inset) fired shell,[72] key to the "reddish vein about a foot thick"[73] of fabulously rich gold ore which they stumbled upon nearby.

Man-made lakes now cover much of the Salt River where Barry Storm (inset) himself scouted far and wide after the proper canyon leading to Gonzales' Mexican mine.

8. GONZALES' MEXICAN MINE

The youthful but hungry-looking Mexican, who called himself Ramón Peralta y Gonzales, had obviously endured an exhausting journey. He was gaunt and ragged and the roan horse with thoroughbred lines, which had been his only transportation from California, was gaunt and nearly spent. And the both of them were streaked with dry desert dust. But to Charles M. Clark,[59] who was the telegrapher at Maricopa, neither man nor beast had suffered anything which couldn't be cured by rest and good food. So in this year of 1874, before the Southern Pacific had laid its tracks through the isolated Arizona villages and Ed Schieffelin had staked out his fabulous Tombstone claims, Clark offered the Mexican food for himself and the trade of two Indian ponies for the exhausted roan horse.

Gonzales accepted both for it was a fair bargain. And then after a few days rest he went to work around the village making adobe building bricks instead of traveling on. In fact, he must have intended to stay for he informed his people in Sonora of his whereabouts by letter. But within the month he had received an urgent reply, informing him that his father was on the verge of death and asking him to return home immediately. This, he explained to Clark, was the only reason why he must leave such a promising country and such helpful friends. And he showed Clark the letter, and regretfully vanished for the first time.

The second time Gonzales appeared in Maricopa then he had beyond doubt just come from his home in Sonora, as he told Clark, some months later. And again he was even more fatigued than before, and the pony which he had ridden far and hard was beyond salvage. But this time, Gonzales babbled, he had a map to gold mines, and he needed help to find them.

Maricopa was a lonely spot, a pinpoint in a vast desert sea largely under the domination yet of savage Apache warriors. So Clark didn't mind making conversation when the chance offered. And conversation with anyone who thought he knew where gold mines were located was always of high interest after the way that The Dutchman was keeping the whole territory in a lather of excitement.

"You mean you want a grubstake then," Clark said. "But how am I to know that you really have directions to gold mines? You haven't been in these parts long, you know."

"That is true," Gonzales conceded. "In fact, I have just returned from Sonora where my father died. And you remember the letter about it, calling me home. My father's name was Manuel Peralta and he told me that many years ago in his youth, before there were **Americanos** here, he had taken much placer gold from the **Rio Salado** near the mountains containing **"La Sombrera"** peak across the river from a mountain of four peaks. He told me that he had discovered also, but secretly, much more such gold nearby in a canyon which he called **Fresco,** enough to make many mines. He drew me a map to this gold before he died, and I have come to get it."

"A map?" Clark repeated.

And his interest suddenly shot up to fever heat with this choice bit of information. For he was suddenly remembering that it was only three years ago that Andy Starr[53] had reported how a dying man named Jacobs had stumbled out of that same region of the hat-shaped peak babbling a wild story about finding a Spanish bonanza with a Mexican map obtained in Sonora. And hadn't even The Dutchman said that his gold came from an abandoned Spanish mine. Perhaps there was a connection!

"Let me see this map then," Clark exclaimed excitedly. "Maybe I'll grubstake you at that."

"But, no," almost snarled Gonzales. "I do not wish anyone to see the map."

"Then I'll not help you," Clark said cagily.

And so it was only with the most obvious reluctance and when he saw that he could expect no help otherwise that Gonzales finally produced his map. And he kept it firmly clenched in his own two hands while he allowed Clark to take a brief look at it.

Clark saw that it was an outline sketch of the Four Peaks on the north and of Weaver's Needle on the south with a line drawn between to cross the Salt River midway between the locating peaks. It was very crudely made, obviously from memory. But at the point where the locating line between peaks crossed the river was the tributary **Cañon Fresco** running south from the river itself to branch into an east fork and south fork. At the branching were four crosses and that magic word, **minas**!

"Mines!" translated Clark excitedly. "But this **Cañon Fresco** —is it meant to be the first canyon above the crossing of the locating line over the river or below. It's hard to be sure of which from this rough sketch. Or is it exactly on the line?"

"Ah, **senor**," said Gonzales. "That is the secret key which only I know."

"Will you tell me?" asked Clark.

"You'll help me with a horse and provisions and a rifle to save me from Apaches?" countered Gonzales narrowly.

"I'll stake you if you let me copy the map and tell me the key," Clark exclaimed feverishly, thinking that the map must indeed be to mines in the Superstitions such as The Dutchman had found. And in his excitement he missed the look of cunning thoughtfulness which passed momentarily over Gonzales' swarthy features.

"As you can see," explained Gonzales at last, "the **Cañon Fresco** containing the gold lies upon the same side of the river as **"La Sombrera"** peak. It is the first canyon **above** where the line between peaks crosses the river."

Thus the trade was made, and after Clark had hastily copied the map, the son of Manuel Peralta rode off toward the

Superstitions upon Clark's horse, with Clark's rifle in the boot under his leg and with Clark's grub in his saddlebags, just twenty-seven years after his father had gone to Sonora.

Crossing the desert toward the northeast then Gonzales rode on past the western end of the mountains, through the pass at Apache Gap and on to the Salt River beyond. And then he merely followed up the riverbank until he had encountered the two old **arrastres** near the site of his father's gold. Near the site, too, of the mapped **Cañon Fresco**!

But the arrastres were not all that he found!

There were human bones scattered about, still partially covered by the last disintegrating remnants of clothing, and among the bones skulls that were horribly naked and bleached a deathly white by the merciless desert sun—human skulls that seemed to grin in sardonic mockery at the golden secret they silently guarded. Nearby were the tumbled remains of an ancient camp.

Gonzales passed by these grisly remains of the twenty-six year old massacre wonderingly, and went over to the camp. And there with a gasp of amazement he saw behind the tumbled ruins of the breastworks where Pedro's unlucky men upon the river had made their last stand a number of neat little piles of glittering, yellow gold shining through rotted hide sacks—concentrates from Pedro's mines back in the Superstitions.

This was indeed rare good fortune which Manuel Peralta had not foretold upon his deathbed. For with such a treasure Gonzales could live a full life among his own kind in California. And no need now to seek further up the **Cañon Fresco** which his father had mapped though that golden canyon was indeed right at hand, running southeast from the little valley later called Mormon Flat. It was, in fact, Tortilla Creek which trended east and the **minas** location was either near one of the south tributary canyons which came into it four or five miles above or was yet several miles further up where other south forks branched off to match the map's description. For instead of being the first canyon above the locating line between peaks which crossed the Salt River, **Cañon Fresco** was actually the first one **below**. But could one be blamed for telling such a little lie under such harsh circumstances?

And now all Gonzales had to do was fill up the cans and sacks which he had brought along with the glittering golden grains. So he returned, much to Clark's surprise, to Maricopa a week or so ahead of his schedule.

Clark really became excited now when he saw with his own eyes this golden proof, so he thought, of the mapped way to fortune. For Gonzales shared with him a large baking powder can full of gold dust[39]—then in the excitement, and without disclosing the full truth of the fortune which he had found, he persuaded Clark to sell him the horse, for a paltry three hundred dollars, upon which that fortune was even then loaded, with which to travel on, he said, to relatives in California.

Many years later Clark tried to find the source of the gold which he had shared, then both he and his son searched but still unsuccessfully. Once they thought Fish Creek might have been the mapped **Cañon Fresco** since its entrance into the river was almost upon the line between peaks. Later they decided that if Gonzales had lied that he must have said just the opposite from the truth. So they did considerable placering in LaBarge Creek with small success, entirely overlooking the fact that the deeper, longer drainage of Tortilla Creek, into which LaBarge Creek ran near its mouth at Mormon Flat actually made the latter a tributary and not the real **Cañon Fresco** first below the locating line.

To this day Tortilla Creek is still unrecognized as the true **Cañon Fresco**, whether or not the Peters Canyon or some other fork further above marks the site of **minas**. In fact, more than one prospecting party has found placer gold above and near the falls where shady cottonwoods, sheer cliffs and ever-tumbling waters match the Spanish name. Here, too Russel Perkins[75] of

Tortilla Flat reported finding huge ash piles and other remains of an obviously large encampment, while Clark's son, Carl[59] himself stumbled upon a piece of hexagon drill steel sharpened Spanish-style in the form of a pointed, four-edged spearhead instead of the chisel bit of today.

But though Clark never learned of it, Gonzales reappeared in the Superstitions again in 1930. This time he came up from the southern desert, apparently making for Weaver's Needle. But he was very old and climbing was hard, and in some way he missed his course slightly so that he came into upper LaBarge Canyon near Roy Bradford's[76] camp where the sheer crags of Bluff Springs Mountain effectively blocked any view of **La Sombrera**. And he casually asked Bradford to direct him to a black-topped hill which lay north of a hat-shaped peak somewhere in the vicinity. He was Gonzales, he said, and he was seeking old mines which relatives had once worked.

Bradford was all excitement at once then for he had recently found at the junction of Bluff Springs and Needle Canyons hardly a mile away a huge suguaro into which seventeen stones had been embedded high up as though shot there from a nearby mine blast. So he was digging, he thought, even then upon the site of those very mines. And he bluntly pressed Gonzales for further details.

At this unwarranted interest of course Gonzales promptly fell into a wary silence. Then Bradford, seeing that no more information was forthcoming and not wishing to disclose the site of his own digging, told the old Mexican that the mountain he sought lay yet several miles further north. And Gonzales thanked him and again vanished into thin air, never to return.

But with him vanished forever Bradford's one chance at fortune!

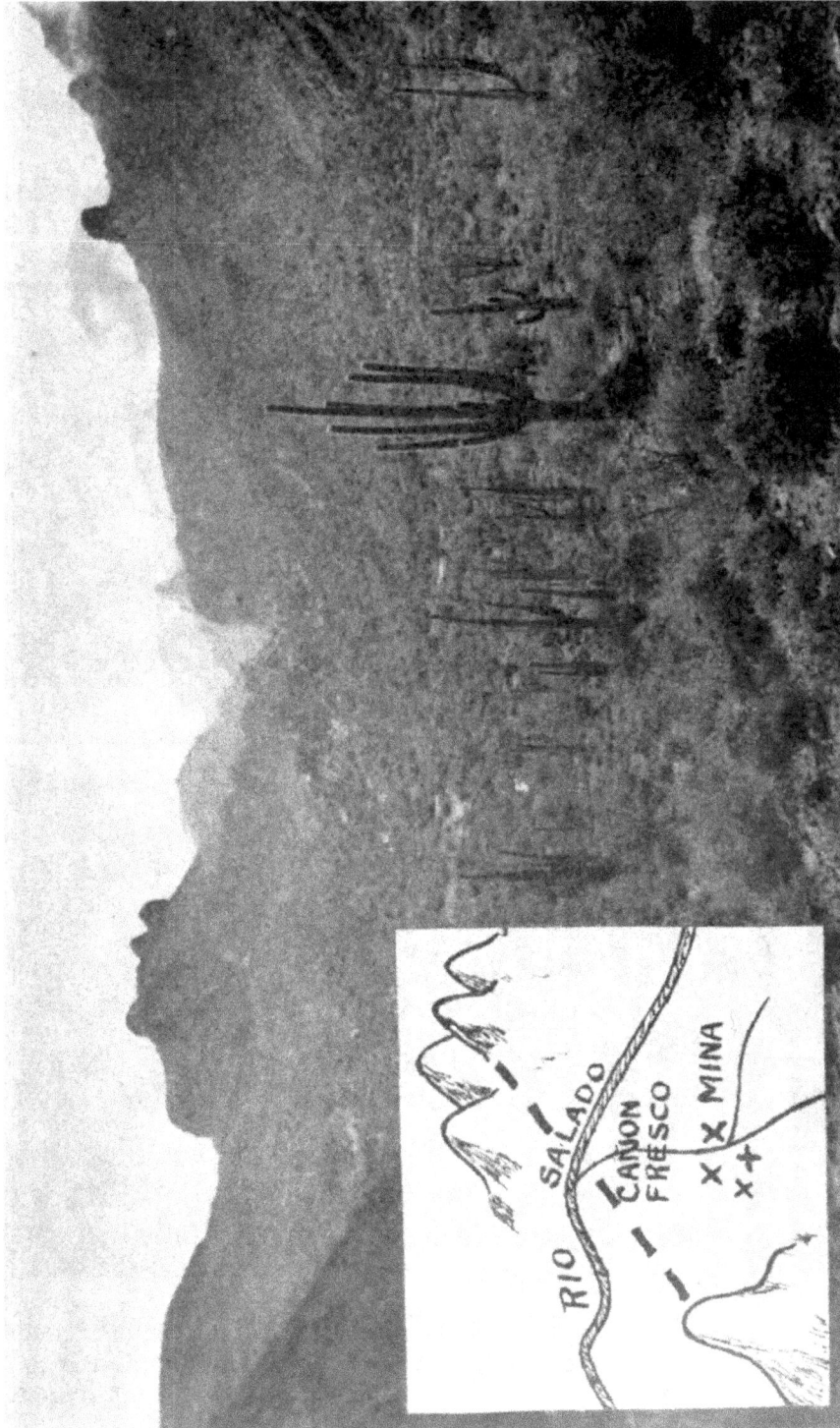

Tortilla Creek beyond (middle distance) its Peters Canyon junction is thought to be the locality of Gonzales' Mexican mine located in the (inset) mapped **Cañon Fresco.**[59]

Geronimo Head mountain, playground of sardonic thunder gods, hides the famed Apache chief's gold[70] somewhere across (below) LaBarge Canyon where (arrow) John Carrol[77] later took a small fortune from a now hidden bonanza vein.

9. MOUNTAIN TREASURES

The soldier liked his whiskey raw and out of a bottle. A man-sized bottle!

"The Irish in me," he grinned, turning the little leather pouch upside down and spilling out a golden cascade of rough, yellow grains upon John Carrol's[77] store counter.

Carrol looked at the glittering heap, obviously mortared from solid quartz by hand, and an answering gleam warmed his eyes. For this had been going on for some months now. And in the early 1900's a Mesa storekeeper had only one worry about selling liquor to Fort McDowell soldiers: could they pay? This one always did eventually, and in gold! But from where?

Carrol knew that soldiers who spent their time off duty in prospecting were no novelty. The novelty was in one of them finding gold. So this soldier was an exception and Carrol let him remain an exception even when, months later still, he was drinking up his gold faster than he was digging it. Then one day the word was out that a whole regiment from the Fort was to be transferred to Montana.

The next time the soldier came into Carrol's store Carrol asked for payment in full of the quite large bill. And since the soldier at the moment was short in gold and long on a thirst for whiskey before his impending transfer, to say nothing of the possibility of having his pay attached, "a sporting proposition" was inevitable. Yes, Carrol might call the bill even and throw in some traveling whiskey to boot for the location of the gold ore. For it must be of bonanza richness if an amateur like the soldier could have mortared out the amount by hand that he had. But it had better be there! A letter could follow the soldier's commander even to Montana. And so a trade was made for the still-phantom vein.

It was in the Superstitions, the soldier said, and up a main canyon running south from near Mormon Flat. An idea of about where could be obtained by going to the parade ground at Fort McDowel, standing at the flagpole there and then running an imaginary line to the pointed tip of Weaver's Needle, visible in the distance. Where the line crossed the main canyon would be about the right location. The vein itself was in a small arroyo coming into the canyon from the west bank near this point. But probably Carrol could still find the soldier's tracks there.

John Carrol took this good advice as soon as he conveniently could and actually obtained enough gold to cause him to sell his business and retire for years afterwards. In fact, on his last trip to the vein Carrol took his son along, and they rode horseback for a bit over an hour up what could only have been LaBarge Creek. Then they reached a well mineralized region of hills on the west bank made reddish by oxidizing iron. There they tied their horses and cooked a lunch, leaving behind to mark the spot a frying pan, coffee pot and some cotton sugar sacks in which they had carried supplies.

From this point they climbed up the west bank into one of the numerous arroyos a short distance to where a small quartz vein lay partly exposed. Then from the hanging wall of the vein, which seemed to be about half metal, a mixture of variously colored flint quartz, hematite and gold, the elder Carrol obtained the small fortune which made life easy for many years after. And then the vein apparently vanished into thin air— was probably covered again by errosion debris from above. For twelve years later young Jim Carrol[77] returned alone, easily refound the lunch camp in LaBarge Canyon but never again the small, fabulous vein of gold ore he had once seen. To this day it remains hidden though occasionally travelers through the region report finding a lone piece or two of the flint-like, brightly-colored quartz, heavy with both iron and gold, that seems to be breaking loose at infrequent intervals from a nearby hillside vein.

But there is at least one other vein in the region of reddish hills where large surface masses of low-assay gold ore yield "colors" to occasional prospectors. And it is not hidden, this bonanza vein of rose quartz, for it has already produced many bars of crude gold bullion though it has not been worked by white men for well over a century. It is upon the mountain now called Geronimo Head which rises sheer and ragged a thousand feet or more to form the east wall of LaBarge Canyon directly across from the reddish hills.

Geronimo Head, which encloses a rugged area of about six square miles, was once, said the Apache chief whose name it bears, a favorite hiding place when hard pressed by pursuing soldiers—and the once or twice source of the gold which financed many hard-fought campaigns against the invading white men who were stealing Indian lands and Indian living. Somewhere in its bewildering maze, which would baffle even a mountain goat, and stretching south from Tortilla Flat for over three miles into the wild Superstitions, is a naturally hidden, sunken box canyon, a veritable slit in solid rock, probably fault formed and errosion cut. The greatest of Apache chiefs, Geronimo[70], himself, has said that it is there. And Geronimo has never lied.

Many decades before even Geronimo was born that hidden canyon had been stumbled into by a party of armor-clad Spaniards, one of the small bands that unknown to history marched and countermarched over the hazardous eighteen century wilderness in search of god. There they found gold in a rose quartz vein so rich that crude hand mortaring alone sufficed to work the rock. And in the course of a few months they had a low tunnel following the vein into the mountain from the sunken valley, a comfortable camp and a small rock smelter near a spring that broke out of solid rock nearby. It did not matter that they had to go in and out of the hidden valley on a rope hung down from above. But this fact was their undoing—and the foolish use of all their gunpowder for mining!

Apache scouts had long since discovered their presence there. And a party of warriors bided their time unseen in the nearby mountains.   Then finally when the Spaniards had no more powder left for either mining or their dreaded wheellock muskets and were preparing to leave with their golden treasure the Indians encircled the rim of the sunken valley and leisurely destroyed the unlucky invaders to the last man with volleys of arrows and boulders rolled from the high cliffs above.

Lost men, lost gold!

But the gold could not be destroyed.   The great glittering pile of crudely shaped bullion was stacked like so much cordwood inside the tunnel.   And there it still remains, many Apaches know to this day though they will never tell the white men who had so often cheated them.

Geronimo once scornfully admitted after his capture that this same sunken valley somewhere in the towering maze of the mountain that bears his name was the place where he had vanished from pursuit on more than one occasion.   And history records the near-scandal at Fort Sill, Oklahoma when at last Geronimo had been imprisoned there in 1886—and there plotted for his escape!   Gold was the mainspring of that plot, gold from an ancient Spanish mine known only to trusted Apaches. And yet the gold which had been mined there was only as a grain of sand to the desert of gold still left in the rose quartz vein.

A certain spring[78] at the foot of the monutain in a deep canyon was the key to the treasure, Geronimo derisively told a fellow prisoner one day, after his escape plot was blocked. For that spring was really fed by the one high up in the sunken valley.   By following the water in its devious meandering over and through a mountain of solid rock a white man might come again upon the mine and its horde of gold.

Once in the 1920's that fabulous valley was seen by Charlie Morgan[79] of Phoenix while on a mountain climbing jaunt up the Apache Trail.   Morgan said he even climbed down into it on a lowered rope and the found a twisting cave—cut at last by errosion—through the lower enclosing wall of the sunken valley and through which he could just barely squeeze to get outside again upon the mountainside. Morgan had stumbled upon the valley by accident for there was nothing to indicate its sunken presence, he said, until he had actually come upon the rim of it. Its location, he estimated, was between four and five miles easterly of the prehistoric burial mounds and walled-up terraces in the Superstitions now known as Garden Valley[80], from which he had hiked. But Morgan, in his hurry to find a way out again from the sunken valley into which he had dropped, gave only the scantiest attention to the ancient camp remains and an eighteenth century Spanish wheellock which he had found lying upon the ground there. For after all such relics of Spanish explorations in the Southwest are not uncommon. So Morgan did not find out about and never saw the fabulous vein and golden treasure so near at hand!

There is other treasure, too, in the Superstitions, and not so far off across the mountains as the crow flies. It is Indian treasure also—a veritable hill of silver ore which must be almost solid metal in places, a series of errosion-cut galena pillars located somewhere in the bed of lower Queen Creek which sweeps down from the southeastern slopes of the mountains onto the vast Arizona desert beyond. The silver is covered now by flood-debris but at least once in the last half century a desert flood had uncovered it temporarily. And perhaps it, too, had once been worked by Spaniards for several prospectors have publicly reported finding the remains of a small Spanish smelter and silver ore slag in the vicinity.

The Apaches[81] called it the "hidden silver antelope" because, doubtless, of the shape of a gleaming metallic pillar. And when David Hawkins' uncle[82], prospecting out of Phoenix in 1890, came upon an Apache youth pinned by a broken leg under his horse and nursed him back to health, the youth's father told him about it. But it took Hawkins' uncle just an even half century to find it in 1940.

"A mountain of native silver and lead, thousands of tons," he told Hawkins. "You can take an axe and chop it. It seemed unreal but there it was finally uncovered where I had walked over it often."

By that time the old prospector "had it made." And so when he had gone east to retire he had looked up his nephew in Illinois on the way and had given him a map "made with compass from a sure known point" on the day that he had found the silver uncovered. Two weeks later he had gone back "mark for mark and found nothing but sand." And he explained, "Then I knew what Apaches meant by this 'hidden' business. The silver was underneath."

But it was gold that Wallace McDonald[83] found unwittingly in 1916 as he was herding cows down Needle Canyon, after having just stuffed his chaps pockets there with stones to throw at the steers. For he still had a few left when he rode into Goldfield that evening. And after a drink all around he was ready to rib the miners a little.

"If you fellows want to see real ore, take at look at this," he said, producing a rock that he had picked up that day. He, himself, he had always said, could fall over gold and never know it.

"Son," exclaimed one of the miners with bulging eyes. "This here **is** gold ore—lousy rich!"

"Gold?" echoed McDonald, flabbergasted.

And the joke was on him, for search as he might he could never find its source.

The thunder gods keep their secrets well!

10. WAGONER'S LOST LEDGE

In the early 1890's while Fred Mullins[84] was still driving the Pinal-Mesa stage one of his passengers, known only as Wagoner[24], would often ride out onto the desert from Pinal and then vanish for weeks at a time. Sometimes, Mullins said, Wagoner would drop off at the western end of the Superstitions and then head north through Apache Gap to prospect across the Salt River. But always, sooner or later, Mullins woud run into him again somewhere along the road, waiting for a ride back to Pinal.

Wagoner, it was said, was from "back East" and a "lunger" who had to stay outdoors and in the sunshine if he wished to keep alive. So he was always on the move, prospecting here and there, carrying a blanket roll and a suitcase full of provisions. Then after one of these trips, on a day in 1894, Wagoner found himself on the north side of the river and out of grub.

It was a long, hungry hike back past the western end of the Superstitions to the stage road toward Pinal. But an extra hungry day might be saved, Wagoner decided, by striking straight across country through the mountains and then either catching the stage again on the desert beyond or at least winding up within easy hiking distance of Pinal. So Wagoner crossed the river at Mormon Flat, hiked up the Apache Trail to Tortilla Flat and then headed due southeast up Tortilla Creek.

For some hours afterwards he followed the creek bed between high cliffs and steep slopes until at last he had reached the flatter country on the east side of Tortilla Mountain. Then he turned due south through the lower hills which, he knew, separated him from the head of LaBarge Canyon and a trail there which went on down the southern slopes of the Superstitions through Red Tank Canyon to Whitlow's Ranch near the stage road to Pinal beyond. It should have been an easy day's hike for a man used to hiking. But after traveling all day Wagoner finally reached LaBarge Canyon only to discover that he had misjudged his direction slightly and was now a couple of miles lower and further west than he had expected.

Night was upon him now, making it difficult to travel further even if he had found the trail. So Wagoner went on down LaBarge Canyon another mile by staying in the center where the walking was open and comparatively easy until he had found a spring of water about three miles due east of Weaver's Needle.

When daylight came again, Wagoner discovered that he was almost due north of Miner's Needle, and once more he decided to simply cut across country to the southeast and get back onto the trail below Red Tank Canyon. And he headed down over the broken hills to the east of Miner's Needle—and almost within the hour stumbled upon a rose quartz ledge outcropping on a southern slope. Immediately he knocked off a few pieces with his prospector's pick and found that the pinkish, glassy rock was literally studded with nuggets of bright, yellow gold!

Here were all his dreams come true—freedom from want and worry, from having to beg strangers for grubstakes, freedom to pursue his easy-going nomadic life as he pleased. For gold, the price of food, fresh air and sunshine, was also the price of life to Wagoner. And breaking off a few pounds of the bonanza rock to put in his suitcase, he hiked blithely on into Pinal, his hunger all but forgotten.

From that time on for months Mullins observed that Wagoner invariably left the stage in the vicinity of Whitlow's Ranch and as invariably caught it again there a few days or a week or so later. And now he also had two brand new, and vastly expensive, solid leather suitcases in which to carry his groceries and effects. But instead of being empty when Wagoner flagged him down for a ride back to Pinal the twin suitcases, which Mullins helped many times to hoist up to the baggage rack on top, were even heavier returning.

About this time, too, there began to be some rumors in Pinal to the effect that Wagoner was now consistently cashing in large amounts of free gold which he had obviously hand crushed and separated from rose quartz rock. And then occasionally there would be an additional passenger who rode out from Pinal and upon one pretext or another would disembark shortly after Wagoner had left the stage.

At first Mullins merely thought that Wagoner had found a likely prospect at last which he was trying to keep hidden from one or more of his numerous grubstakers who all seemed to be trying to trail him to it. And he wasn't much surprised one day when these extra passengers started confiding that Wagoner always hiked a short ways up canyon from Whitlow's Ranch where he camped out under a willow tree. Then always at a moment when he was unwatched he would vanish abruptly toward the Superstitions with the suitcases slung over his shoulders on straps.

All of this mystery would have been less interesting had not Wagoner at the same time been literally working himself to death in running back and forth between Pinal and the Superstition Mountains. But he explained it all himself one day when he appeared, pale and sick this time, and asked Mullins to hoist the bags up alone. He had finished a certain job now, he remarked. And Mullins, agreeing that he should certainly take things easier from the looks of him, almost strained his own husky back getting the twin suitcases aboard. What was in them, he asked Wagoner, that they should be so heavy?

"Look and see," Wagoner invited. "This is my last trip anyway."

And Mullins opened one of the bags to find it stuffed with glittering, hand-picked gold ore of bonanza grade!

"Looks like you got it made, sure enough," Mullins exclaimed excitedly. "But many's the time I gave you a free lift when you were broke. How about telling a friend."

And he persuaded Wagoner to tell him the whole story of his accidental discovery and how he had been returning to it, wiping out his trail each time with a piece of sacking which he had drug along behind. Wagoner even obligingly made Mullins a detailed map[24] showing the way back up Red Tank Canyon into upper LaBarge Canyon and around a picacho butte. He explained, too, that he had always covered the rose quartz outcropping with rocks and brush whenever he had left it, and in addition this last time he had planted a circle of trees around it to grow into a permanent marker in case he should ever want to return. And now he was going to vanish from Pinal with the fortune which he had accumulated and take life easy somewhere for a change. Then vanish he did.

Fred Mullins tried to use his map but he could never quite find the right place. Later, in the early 1900's, a man named Pinkey[24], who said that he had once been one of Wagoner's "partners" or grubstakers, showed up at the Quarter-Circle-U Ranch below Miner's Needle, with a letter and a map signed by Wagoner and dated twenty years before. The letter indicated that Wagoner had actually ended up in a Tucson hospital within a year or so after he had vanished from Pinal. He then for some unknown reason had sent the map to Pinkey of all his partners with instructions to meet him near "the board house" (Whitlow's Ranch) for a last trip since he was not expected to live long. But Wagoner died instead, and Pinkey came just twenty years too late for his rendezvous with fortune—to the wrong house.

Many years later still Ray Howland[85] of Mesa came in 1933 upon what was probably Wagoner's key in LaBarge Canyon without realizing the possible significance—two pieces of fabulously rich rose quartz gold ore beside a faint trail, markers perhaps to the proper turning off place and waiting fortune!

Tortilla Flat, almost lost in the immensity of space along the famed Apache Trail, marks the entrance of Tortilla Creek into the Superstitions where, a day's travel south, Wagoner found his rich rose quartz ledge of bonanza gold ore.

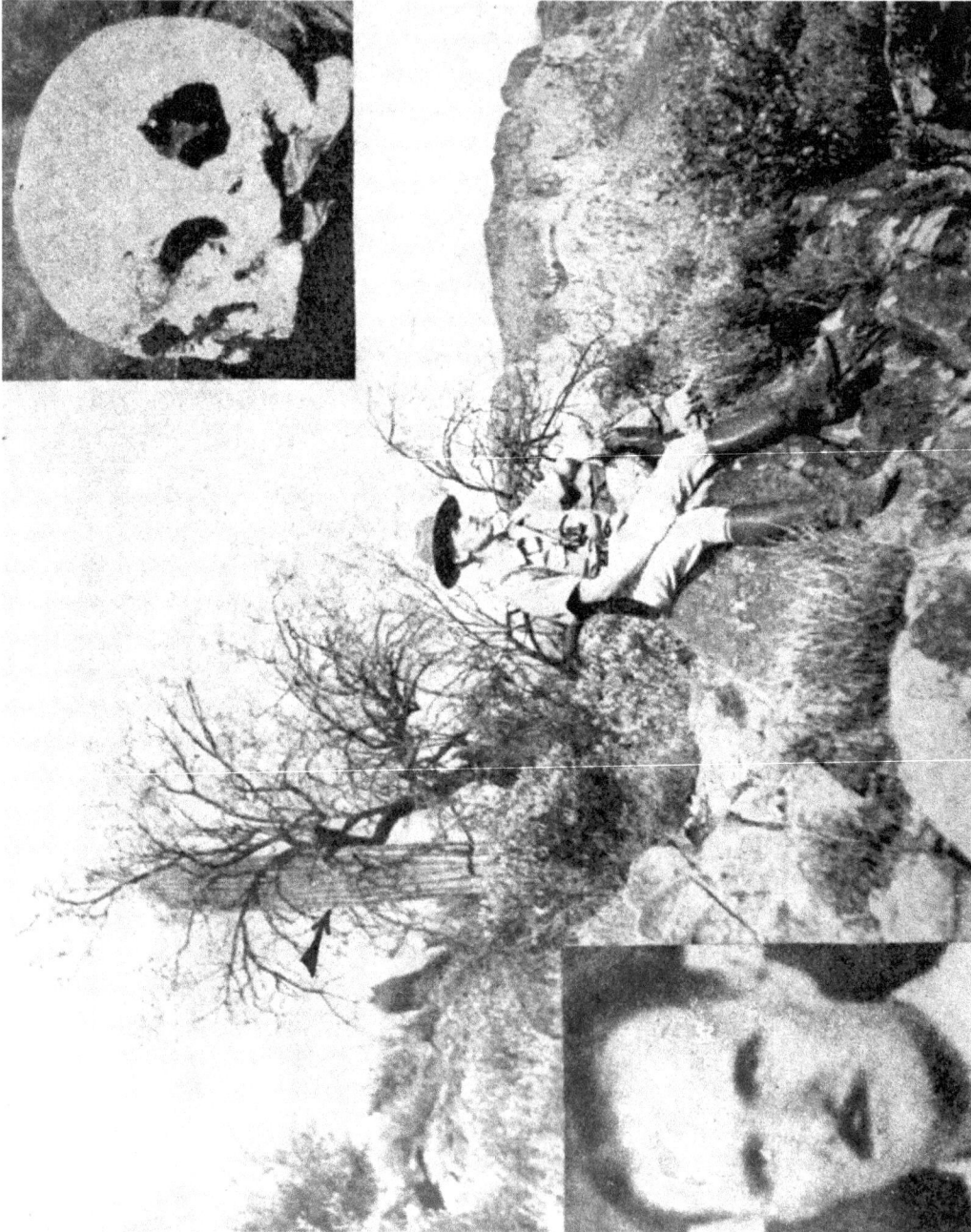

Barry Storm sitting upon the ledge around which Adolph Ruth's remains[41] were found after (top inset) his bullet-pierced skull had disclosed a murderer's game for treasure. In inset below is Erwin C. Ruth who had procured the authentic Peralta map which led to his father's still-unsolved death.

11. RUTH'S SPANISH MINE

Adolph Ruth, it is generally conceded by those who knew him best, had actually identified the location of one of the Peralta mines in 1931—before the thunder gods' curse overtook him! For found in his own handwriting, in Latin, was a note which he had hidden under a flap of his checkbok. It said significantly: "I came, I saw, I conquered. About 200 feet across from cave."

Nor was Ruth at all as inexperienced in treasure hunting as many had thought because of the natural naivette which had developed with his nearly sixty years of age. Indeed, he had successfully found one of the Lost Pegleg Mines in California some years before with the aid of an old map, and had broken his leg in falling into the ancient, worked-out shaft. He had hunted other treasures too during many vacations from his Civil Service clerical positionin Washington, D. C. and had long since become expert in deciphering the old charts which he continually accumulated. But now he had obtained the last of the original Peralta maps and all of the information which went with it.

"I have a Spanish map," he often naively declared upon his arrival in Arizona[87]. "My son, Erwin, obtained it first-hand from a descendant of the original Peraltas in 1912. And I know it will show me the way to their lost mines."

In a letter[15] Erwin C. Ruth verified his father's statements with the following extract: "The person I received the map from was a former Mexican consul to the United States by the name of Gonzales, a grandson of a Peralta. He claimed that the foundation of his family's wealth derived from old Peralta gold mines in Arizona."

And subsequent investigation through diplomatic channels revealed that Gonzales was none other than the son of a daughter of the original Manuel Peralta with whom Erwin Ruth had become friendly while working in Mexico at the time. Gonzales was executed in 1912 for his part in a revolution, the circumstances indicating that he had given the old Peralta heirloom to young Ruth in payment for Ruth's seeing to the safety of his family upon his impending death. So at long last did Manuel's map come to light! And Erwin Ruth had passed the map on to his treasure-hunting father who now, nineteen years later, was anxiously awaiting a chance to use it in the Superstitions!

In fact, for some weeks now the elder Ruth had been waiting at Barkley's Quarter-Circle-U Ranch on the southern slopes of the mountains. For who would be a better guide than the hard-bitten cowman who had himself spent a near lifetime there.

But while Ruth was waiting, he was talking. Talking too much, too naively to anyone who would listen. Talking of the fabulous mine he would surely find with his genuine map, of the glittering gold and shiny ore that would soon be his alone; telling it all to Adam Stewart and the rest of Barkley's neighbors, to the cowboys who came and went, to the prospectors and treasure hunters who used Barkley's ranch for a jumping off place. And of all who heard the sly "Mr. X^{88}" alone recognized the region in which Ruth said the lost mines lay, was intimately enough acquainted with that rough topography to see his chance for fortune, must have been even then planning to acquire the Peralta map, and laid his ground work well by pretending to befriend Ruth—before he packed back into the mountains himself to wait. . . .

Small wonder then that W. A. "Tex" Barkley was regarding the aged mine hunter on that hot June morning of 1931 with more pity than enthusiasm. He had done a little treasure hunting himself for amusement, had once found the crumbling ruins of a Spanish-built stone house, and had seen many such men as Ruth vanish into the bewildering maze of desolate canyons beyond, never to return. Perhaps, shrewdly enough, he suspected just about what would happen should Ruth be allowed to wander into those mountains alone with his Peralta map—after having practically invited the whole countryside to murder him for it! So Barkley agreed to give Ruth safe guidance himself in a few days, after he had first attended to some pressing business in town. And he issued orders to his cowboys not to allow Ruth to enter the mountains until his return[89].

But a day passed, and another. And Ruth, growing ever more restless with each fleeting hour, decided at last that he could not longer await Barkley's return. And he went around to First Water on the northwestern side of the mountains where two of the itinerant cowboys whom Barkley occasionally hired, L. F. Purnell and Jack Keenan, were working.

"You know I have a Peralta map that will show me exactly where the mines are located," he said. "Take me into the mountains and I'll see that you are well paid when I find them. If you won't guide me then I am going alone for I know that I have the key to a great fortune."

And Purnell and Keenan, regarding the old man with his crippled leg and walking stick in astonishment, saw at once that they had no choice in spite of Barkley's orders.

"We'll take you into the mountains and help you make a camp near water where you'll be safe,"they said. "But first tell us what section you are looking for so we'll know where to find you if you get lost."

Then again, as he had many times before, Ruth loquaciously detailed one of his chief clues, a canyon junction which anyone familiar with the Superstitions should have recognized instantly, that of Bluff Springs and Needle Canyons—the one running almost north and south from Weaver's Needle with high cliffs flanking it upon the eastern side, and the other, a tributary, coming into it from the east almost at right angles along the northern base of a high mountain near which the Peraltas had once had a mining camp—a singlularly accurate description for one who had never seen it! Above this canyon junction somewhere Ruth said that he would find more exact secret clues to the mines' locations.

Purnell and Keenan loaded Ruth's meager equipment upon a pack animal then and rode him into Willow Springs in West Boulder Canyon. And there they left him alone on June 14, 1931, promising to return in exactly ten days with more supplies[90].

But Ruth was not alone with his fabulous map! For the deadly "Mr. X" undoubtedly trailed him everywhere he went for days until he had decided that the mine hunter was really alone and unwatched by anyone else—the same "Mr. X" who had shot at other treasure seekers before and since and who was cunning enough not to walk on trails[91] but beside them so his distinctively small footprints would not be seen. And then adroitly, by apparent accident perhaps, he met Ruth openly, agreed to show him the canyon junction he wanted to find, beguiled him with talk of the Spanish relics he had himself discovered, and must have indeed offered the facilities of a nearby camp and probably the use of a burro. And the naive Ruth, taking his friendly help at face value, abandoned his own camp and joined the treacherous "Mr. X"

No one probably will ever know exactly what happened. But once in the right region, the hidden note found in Ruth's checkbook and overlooked by his murderer indicates that Ruth himself had stumbled upon the key marker in Needle Canyon when finally located the point from which his map had been drawn, most probably then tried one after another of the directions pointed out until he came at last to the map and signs upon the cliff face of the Peralta-mapped mountain and then had, with his authentic information, successfully identified at least one of the hidden mine locations.

And being the loquacious, naive old man he was, Ruth couldn't help becoming excited, couldn't help speculating in golden terms upon the incredible riches he might disclose when he had filed his claim and had obtained help to open up the hidden mine that he alone knew about. But if Ruth could find a mine with the map he must have refused to show, then "Mr. X" could too! So he shot the unsuspecting mine hunter in the head. For it would be too late if he allowed Ruth to obtain help and safely stake out his claim. And "Mr. X" was a dead shot, knew he was a dead shot and probably to this day still boasts of that ability.

Indeed, no one but the ruthless "Mr. X," whose mind even then was twisted by greed for a fabulous, golden treasure which for years perhaps he had failed to find himself though he often encountered tantalizing clues to prove its nearby presence, could have been so deadly certain that he would obtain in Ruth's Peralta map the one missing clue. No one else could have so easily taken advantage of a previous acquaintanceship and, without a nearby camp and pack animals, been able to have maintained himself in that particular region at that particular time long enough and with the necessary knowledge of Ruth's business to have gained both the motive and the opportunity for murder—and the necessity for packing a corpse from where it might have proved embarrassing to the hidden arroyo where it might never had been found.

And so Ruth and his Peralta map vanished.

Later, during the inquiry by authorities, Purnell and Keenan testified that they had returned to Ruth's camp on June 24 with the additional supplies. Then failing to find Ruth there, they alone began a search of the nearby region, hunting until nightfall. By what process of reasoning they did not go at once to the canyon junction where Ruth had indicated he would be cannot be ascertained. Perhaps they had reason to suspect that an "accident" had occurred and did not wish to become involved in the inevitable investigation. For they avoided that particular regin and said never a word about it at the time.

Later still, however, one of them did tell Abe L. Reid, who also sometimes rode for Barkley, what Ruth had disclosed to them. And further verification of the object of Ruth's search was obtained from his son, who wrote in part: "I remember father stating that he knew which way to travel **from the marker**[92]." But at the time, the officers, who had been summoned by C. R. Morse of Apache Junction, knowing nothing of Ruth's destination, failed to discover any traces.

Months later, by one of those accidental combinations of chance upon which murderers can never depend, a Phoenix newspaper[93] and the City Archaeologist dispatched a joint expedition into the Superstitions to investigate ancient Indian ruins. And it had been raining heavily during the early part of December 1931—and washing away bit by bit the loose dirt which covered a hastily buried human skull, was scenting that grisly relic for a dog's keen nose. And the dog even then trotting ahead of the men and out onto the flat at the foot of Bluff Springs Mountain near Ruth's canyon junction!

Suddenly the dog stopped, growling, lifted its muzzle and bounded over to a palo verde tree at the base of a nearby knoll where it alternately howled and pawed at something in a strangely excited manner. And the men, following after, saw a partly exposed skull that had been piered by bullet holes— sufficient evidence of murder! Evidence, too, that "Mr. X" had thought safely hidden, that brought a thought into every mind.

Adolph Ruth!

The skull was taken back to Phoenix and sent to Dr. Ales Hrdlicha at the Smithsonian Institution in Ruth's own Washington, D. C. where it was positively identified. And so once more a search was begun which ended with the finding of the unlucky mine hunter's scattered remains on January 8, 1932.

The posse (left to right: Hassie Cline, Jeff Adams, Gabriel Robles, Ace Gardner, Tex Barkley, Sheriff J. R. McFadden) who found the remains of Adolph Ruth, veteran treasure hunter (shown below) who met mysterious death just when he had struck a hot trail. (Photos courtesy Arizona Republic.)

But once again the murderous "Mr. X" had done his job too well. And when the posse headed by such experienced mountain men as Tex Barkley and Jeff Adams finally ferreted out the remains, they saw at once that the detached head was not the work of wild animals, nor was the scattering of Ruth's bones and effects over an area of seventy-five yards. And where was the little silver plate that had fastened a fracture in Ruth's thighbone together since an accident years before? The screw holes in the bones were there. But most certainly "Mr. X," who was unsuspectingly being posted on developments, who must have been in the vicinity all the while, undoubtedly had returned to remove that identifying piece of silver when it became obvious that his victim's remains would inevitably be found. And at the same time hadn't he carefully wrapped up Ruth's roll leggings to explain the absence of the shoes which he had taken? For after all these months there were comparatively **fresh** tracks to show that Ruth had walked to the spot himself—the tracks of Ruth's shoes which never were found but not the tracks of Ruth's game leg.

Ruth's hat was missing too—along with his Peralta map. Perhaps the map had been hidden in the hatband and both were taken by "Mr. X" **somewhere else** when he had shot Ruth. At least he did not disturb the contents of one of Ruth's **buttoned** shirt pockets, proving by this lack of interest in other of the dead man's valuables that the map was his motive and golden hope.

"Mr. X" still goes free for mere suspicions are not convicting proof. But unknown to him in 1931 old Ruth had erased from his map in the interest of secrecy the instructions for using it. So when "Mr. X" destroyed Ruth he at the same time destroyed the very clues to fabulous fortune which he had hoped to obtain.

And to this day in the vast, wild reaches of the Superstitions the raucous rumble of the thunder gods' sardonic laughter may still be heard!

12. JENKINS' LOST LODE

It is said that once to every treasure hunter comes the chance for great fortune. And perhaps this chance was mine when Bill Jenkins stumbled upon his fabulous gold ore in the Superstitions.

I had known William P. Jenkins, his wife, Marion, and their two girls, Mary Ann and Wilma, ever since their arrival in Phoenix from Maryland. Several times during the spring of 1937 I had accompanied them on picnics, and the stray jars that Marion used in which to carry lunch fixings became the only clue to the rich ledge near which Bill Jenkins found a piece of drift ore August 1. Two days after I had recorded in my diary:

"At Jenkins' home tonight where Bill showed me half a head big piece of gold quartz ore found last Sunday in Superstitions. Free gold visible all through quartz and extremely rich in inclusions of brown oxidized hematite. Apparently from nearby ledge as three sides of rock are weather-worn but fourth side still rough—not too long ago broken loose. Verified by Marion and children along."

And this, I thought, was enough reason for becoming excited and immediately agreeing to locate the ledge. So I obtained that night half of Bill's rock and his story first-hand.

He had driven, he said, out the Apache Trail to a steel bridge across a creek coming into Canyon Lake, had left the car beside the bridge, and then all of them had hiked up-canyon past steep tuffa cliffs to where at last the canyon had widened between lower hills. At this point, about three hours from the car, they came to a curve in the canyon ahead beyond which they could see for the first time the pointed tip of Weaver's Needle in the distance.

Here Marion found a large, bare log near a steep slope leading to a small, flat-topped hill on the canyon's eastern side. And on the log they ate lunch, stuffing papers under-

neath and leaving several jars scattered about. Then, while
Marion and the girls watched, Bill climbed up the slope to
get a full-view look at Weaver's Needle, picking up on the
way a piece of brilliant quartz. Bill carried this rock for well
over an hour, to the hilltop and then back down into the canyon
below where, he knew, Marion would be delighted with it because of its coloring. In fact, he carried it on back to the car,
a considerable job because it was unusually heavy. Then again
curiosity got the best of him and with a large wrench he man-
aged to break it in two—opening an inside that was literally
dazzling with raw, yellow gold!

Even then, none of the Jenkins were particularly impressed because they had never seen gold and anyway "the whole
hillside was covered with the same kind of rock." But I lost
no time in telling them that it was gold, two days later. And
bright and early the next morning assayer John Foreman was
telling me that it would run around $2,000 a ton — bonanza
stuff! So on August 4th I was at Canyon Lake verifying the
Jenkins' story by their car tracks which I found beside the
Willow Creek bridge and by their occasional footprints still
visible in sandy places up-canyon. But that evening, back in
Phoenix I found that my luck was not all good. For during the
day Bill had also taken his piece of ore to the same assayer
and upon discovering its value refused to give me any further
information. That same day, too, Marion, who worked at a
Civil Service position, had been transferred to a Tucson office
and they were moving. So I promised to "lay off" Bill's discovery.

Two years swiftly passed. And everytime I was in Tucson
I made it a point to again verify the story from Marion and
the girls, and try to persuade Bill to change his mind. Many
times Marion and the girls insisted that they could easily find
their way back. But I was blocked from this ideal solution by
Bill's insistence that he planned to follow up his discovery him-

Willow Springs Creek which hides the secret of Jenkins' now-lost ledge of fabulous ore in the vicinity of (inset) a bottle[94] left at their lunch stop and identified by his wife. In large inset is the composite copy of the Jenkins' map[25].

self. Then at last, during August, 1939, Bill agreed to join an expedition the following November after an impending visit with relatives in New York. And I went to San Diego, as recorded October 25, 1939 in the **San Diego Union**[95], to organize the expedition which moved into the Superstitions. But Bill Jenkins never appeared and I backtracked the clues instead which resulted in my Peralta mine discovery[3] of 1940. Over a year later, when I finally found time to look up the Jenkins once more, I learned from Marion that Bill had arrived on schedule to join me—and then had died of heart failure the next day!

Now that my promise was dissolved by Bill's death — as almost incredible as it seemed at the time! — I arrived at an agreement with Marion Jenkins, obtained maps and additional confidential data[25], and succeeded myself in finding during March, 1942 one of the jars[94] which had been left behind in Willow Springs Canyon, and which Marion identified as hers from my description. I had after practically half a decade found their lunch stop and struck a hot trail! But just as a world-wide war made further treasure hunting impossible!

And yet wars do not last forever!

Today, Marion Jenkins, though happily married again, still thinks that she can remember the right way back—and her husband would like to go treasure hunting too! And both girls, grown up meanwhile, Wilma to follow a sailor husband on war duty and Mary Ann awaiting her own call to duty in the Armed Forces, are certain that someday they can retrace their steps to their father's now-lost lode. Perhaps, too, one day soon now I'll be able to resume my own trail to fortune!

That is the dream that never dies!

PART III

ADVENTURE TRAILS

"Why to yon mountain turns the musing eye,
Whose sun-bright summit mingled with the sky?
Why do those cliffs of shadowy tint appear
More sweet than all the landscape smiling near?
'Tis distance lends enchantment to the view
And robes the mountain in its azure hue."

—THOMAS CAMPBELL

Like lonely sentinels guarding a fantastic treasureland the giant saguaros march forever away to infinity along Western desert trails.

1. GOLD IN THE SUPERSTITIONS

I took an anxious breath and refocused my fieldglasses. But it was still yellow gold, glittering brightly in the midday sun.

Excitement fired my blood then like intoxicating wine, shook my hands with a violent trembling. For this was gold-bearing drift rock from some mineralized strata beyond on which lost mines **could** be located—mineralized proof that gold was **in** the Superstitions!

And at long last I had found it after slow months of prospecting around those wild mountains—on the east where towering cliffs and twisted canyon-chasms lifted up into the higher reaches of the rugged Mazatzals, on the south and west where endless Arizona desert flowed away to a dim horizon, on the north where the lazy Salt River separated this traditional domain of Apache thunder gods from the Four Peaks country beyond. At long last! But now . . .

Triumphantly I wiped the sweat from my face, then forced myself to go on calmly up the dry, rocky streambed of Boulder Canyon with fieldglasses glued to my eyes. Thus I examined many feet before me as I walked every pebble magnified to boulder size. And so I came to the bit of glittering rock which might otherwise have remained invisible forever.

I picked it up, saw that it was flint-like quartz speckled with iron pyrite and gold, hefted its unusual weight exultantly in my hand. Bonanza stuff! And fit clue to the long-lost Peralta mines once worked in that vast, bewildering mountain maze. Perhaps, I thought, it was even fit clue to the fantastic, world-famous jewel of wealth, the one of those mines which The Dutchman had refound for himself in the 1870's!

The roseate visions of it thrilled me, then suddenly froze my blood. It was as though the heat had gone from the sun all at once, as though I was sweating, cold and clammy, in a chill wind. And somehow in that exciting moment I had a queer, fleeting impression that unseen, vaguely-felt wraiths were present, that all those others who had gone before—those dead ones! —had gathered in spirit about me. For this was gold stained with Spanish blood, gold cursed by Apache thunder gods, gold in the Superstitions!

And then as strangely the sun was hot once more. And the heat waves shimmered up from furnace-like rock to obscure the jagged, distant crags and sheer, multi-colored cliffs beyond, the misty palos verdes, spiny cholla and odd prickly pear nearer at hand, the giant saguaros with grotesquely twisted arms which seemed to march forever away to infinitely like lonely desert sentinels guarding a fantastic treasureland.

It was a treasureland, I was certain then—a strange, forgotten world of perhaps a hundred square miles set securely apart behind towering ramparts of stone; a miniature frontier which had inadvertantly been bypassed by civilization; a raw, primeval land peopled still with Spanish ghosts and savage gods, trod yet by The Dutchman's restless spirit, haunted forever by all those unhappy phantoms who had sought lost mines only to vanish themselves without a trace. But would I become entwined in this fatal web of disaster that had been a near-century in the making? I most certainly hoped so!

That night back in my desert camp, sitting cross-legged in the flickering light of a mesquitewood campfire, I marked in on my topographic map of the Superstitions all of the north-south trending region in the mountains which Boulder Canyon and its Needle and East and West Boulder Canyons tributaries drained. Then I went over the notes I had previously compiled of nearby mining productions since pioneer days, especially those trending east-west.

First there was the famed ghost mining camp of Goldfield near the western end of the mountains. Officially it had produced $67,000 in gold, unofficially over a million. East of it smaller productions dotted a mile wide straight swath for a distance, became blank in the interior of the Superstitions, then twenty-odd miles eastward continued on again. Here then was a mineralized band, proven upon both eastern and western ends, which localized where it crossed at right angles the north-south Boulder Canyon drainage in which I—and others before me!— had found golden drift rock a definite region of perhaps eight square miles. This, I could be **geologically** sure, was the source of the occasional pieces of ore sometimes found below, the most probable **mineralogical** location of any hidden mines in the mountains, and therefore the most likely region in which to search for clues left behind by the Peraltas and later by The Dutchman himself. It was really that simple!

But this finding of **identifiable** evidence to prove history right would be the hardest task of all. For just as ancient trails could still be followed by the scratch of iron muleshoe upon rock which leaves for the expert eye a slight, rusty streak of oxidizing metal generations later, so must a treasure hunter work only upon the logical theory that no matter where pioneer miners had gone or when they must invariably have left something behind to prove it—trail markers, campsites, lost or discarded equipment, treasure signs and prospecting work.

I would have to locate such evidence, I knew, before I would have either a story or the chance of discovering a lost mine. In fact, such a story would be incredible without verification. And a hidden three or four foot hole in the ground would have to be localized to a much smaller area than eight square miles before it could be found with anything short of a lifetime search. Yet the possibilities were actually thrilling for a treasure hunter **on trail** always becomes fair game to all manner of unscrupulous men who will stop at nothing if the chance for fortune becomes a reality. And a sheriff's posse had less than six years before this hot June night of 1937 gathered up the bones of the last victim who had been murdered for the

Peralta map he had carried just when he had struck a hot trail, a matter nationally publicised but still unsolved. Unsolved, too, were strange disappearances in the Superstitions, mysterious shootings, unsolved the reason for inevitable ill fortune in that unlucky domain of Apache thunder gods.

So in exultant anticipation that night I crawled into my sleeping bag spread out under a mesquite tree and let the distant **yap-yap-yap** of hunting coyotes lull me slowly to sleep.

I do not know how long I had been sleeping. But somehow all at once I knew that I had been hearing for sometime the **clop-clop-clop** of an approaching horseman, for all the world like the incessant beat of a far-away, tom-tom drum. And I awoke suddenly as a cat awakes, sitting bolt upright. For the hoofbeats were making for the red faintness of my campfire.

The stars had dimmed now in the grey pre-dawn so that an erie gloom lay over the desert, a darkness that wasn't dark, a lightness not quite light. And in that weird world of grotesque phantoms half-glimpsed and half-imagined I suddenly spied the huge, darker mass of horse and rider looming like a ghostly shadow from the strange pattern of trees and cacti beyond. Tensely I picked up my revolver, let its cold weight snuggle comfortably into my hand. Then the rider came up to the dying embers of my campfire, and when he saw me sitting up in my sleeping bag with gun in hand he nodded calmly as though that was just the way he had expected to find me.

"Abe Reid's the name," he said finally when I didn't put down my gun. "I got the word you left for me at First Water about wanting lost mine dope."

"Of course," I said, relieved. "Light for breakfast."

Soon we had a tin plate full of flapjacks and bacon apiece and a steaming pot of coffee to scent the air. And as we ate in silent haste I studied him in the strengthening dawn light. For Abe Reid I had never met before though I had learned to know him by name and reputation from my investigation of local history. One of the old-timers of Arizona, an intimate of Indians and pioneers. Lean, hard, ageless, Reid might have been perhaps 40 though he was actually nearer 60.

"Been prospecting?" came his guarded query.

"Yeh," I explained. "I wanted to make sure that there was gold in the Superstitions before I started looking for a lost mine full of it. I need some dope I heard you have."

"Well, I spent two years hunting the Lost Dutchman after the last one got himself killed in there," Reid observed. "There're people who don't want strangers in the mountains."

"Oh, like that," I said calmly enough. "They figure if a lost mine is found they're going to do the finding, eh?"

But I was thinking that here was a direct threat whether meant or not or perhaps subtly passed on by someone unknown. Well, one way of finding adventure was to meet it head-on! And in the same instant I had my gun in hand, as fast a draw as I ever made. I shot from the hip without moving, at the lid of the coffee can lying beside the fire perhaps five paces away, then reholstered my gun as quickly. In the roaring echoes the lid flopped over with a neat hole in it.

Reid looked at me impassively and I saw that there was a gleam of appreciation in his eyes.

"So you mean business," he observed at last noncommittally, and stared absently at the cliffs of the Superstitions rising bold and ragged against the early morning sun.

"That's right," I said. "Got several months of damn hard work in the deal now, what with running down information from here to Mexico, and all the prospecting. What I need now is your dope on the Adolph Ruth murder and the information the Apaches gave you about hiding mines."

"How did you know that?" Reid asked sharply.

"You got excited and talked when you found a hunk of gold ore in 1930," I said. "Part of my business is locating people with long memories."

"Well," explained Reid. "The short of it was that I found the gold on the same mountain that Ruth's Peralta map led him to. The same mountain an old Apache friend described as where he had helped to cover up mines when he was a boy. But you might run into a bullet like Ruth."

"From the guy who shot him?" I wanted to know.

"If he's still around . . . ."

"And wouldn't want me finding things that might put a rope around his neck, eh?"

"You get the idea," Reid said. "Besides, when a man's been too long in the hills . . ." He tapped his head significantly.

"I'll take the chance," I exclaimed, delighted with this opportunity for some excitement. "I have some men coming out to help me soon. We'll want to see this hill of yours. Right now, just one more question." And I fished my copy of the Peralta map out of a pocket.

"All these old maps are usually tied to some dominating peak," I explained. "But any peak will look different from different directions, so by finding where it looks like this outline, I'll get near where the map was made to start with."

"I never thought of that," Reid conceded. "But this shows the way Weaver's Needle looks from Needle Canyon."

"Then it's a hot trail!" I exclaimed in sheer excitement. "Unless Ruth's murderer has already followed it!"

But who cares about a murderer when the subtle ring of lost gold is abroad on the land! Certainly not I!

RIZONA ASSAY C					
#43 St 3-27-40	315 North First Street				
submitted for assay by	Mr. Barry Storm				

SILVER		VALUE (Oz.)	GOLD		VALUE (Oz.)	TOTAL VALUE
Ounces	Tenths		Ounces	Hundths	35.00	Of Gold and Silver
				28.64	$1002.40	

Barry Storm in Boulder Canyon where one of the golden clues he found assayed[96] (above) $1,002.

At Goldfield end of the Superstitions (above) is the mineralized belt which Barry Storm traced eastward to (below) the region of the Peralta-mapped mountain where he is standing near his discovery of the Soldiers' Lost Vein clue which almost cost his life.

2. THUNDER GODS CURSE

John Vall was sleek and heavyset, a little too fat for this desert country, I thought. There was something shifty in his dark, brooding eyes, something which gave me the uncomfortable impression that he was playing a secretive game of his own. He had just come back to the States from a prospecting trip up the Orinoco River at my request, well recommended as a crack geologist. But he was two weeks ahead of the other men I had sent for.

"I'm after lost mines," I told him frankly. "And I have to find first the geological locations of such rich ore possibilities." Then I told him about the two ex-soldiers from Fort McDowel. "I think I have a clue to the region where they found bonanza ore. If I'm right, either the clue itself or the ore somewhere within a half mile supposedly will indicate the right region."

"In either case I can find the ore," he assured me.

I had set up a base camp near First Water, a Quarter-Circle-U Ranch linecamp, from which to work. And mankilling work it was in the hot, broiling sun, we found, when we started out one morning loaded down with grub and sleeping bags in packsacks, canteens and a ten gallon watercan slung on a pole between us jungle style. All day long we pushed on upon an easterly course to intercept the old Military Trail regardless of the terrain, uphill and down, skirting cholla thickets and prickly pear patches, crawling over naked rock so hot it blistered where it touched human skin. Then late in the afternoon we came out abruptly upon a high mesa that ended in unscalable cliffs. And there was Weaver's Needle towering over the region miles away but appearing so close that it seemed we could almost pitch a rock onto those sheer sides.

We shucked our watercan and packs, and just sat there in awe looking at the wild panorama. For there were tumbled hills everywhere which seemed to have been flung about helter-skelter by some giant hand, and in between the hills shadowed canyons and deep slopes in a veritable labyrinth maze. In the distance the horizon was a jagged line, saw-toothed against a cobalt sky.

It seemed strange, I thought, that I should be sitting up there literally upon the edge of nowhere, looking out over a vast and wild country in which history had written an almost unbelievable saga of golden greed and treacherous disaster. And exultantly, I knew, I would soon be walking obscure trails once trod by the Peraltas, The Dutchman and all those others who had come after easy fortune and sooner or later had found violent death instead. But the old military trail would be yet a mile to the east, I saw from my map.

That night we camped in West Boulder Canyon. And as we sat around a campfire of pungent palo verde after a supper of fried quail, I told Vall the story of the soldiers' lost vein, as neat a bit of incredible history as ever really occurred. "So we're sitting right now within two or three miles of it," I concluded. "And if the soldiers got over $500 for the few pieces they brought out to the Silver King — say ten pounds — that would add their ore up to over $100,000 a ton."

Vall's eyes were gleaming darkly in the firelight, though he was trying hard to maintain a sceptical air.

"Then what's the catch?"

"The gambler, Smith, remember," I explained. "After doing murder to get the vein he wouldn't leave it open for someone else to find. I figure he would cover whatever hole he made with the only thing handy, ordinary rocks and dirt. That's the only reason I can see why Forest didn't find it when he had the soldiers' tracks to follow. It wasn't to be seen any more."

"What chance have we got then?" Vall asked sceptically.

"Just this; something so simple no one thought of it in spite of the soldiers telling the whole Silver King camp how they chanced upon the vein—by chasing a deer they jumped up along the trail," I said, getting my notebook from my pack and taking out a clipping. "Here's a photograph of the .52 caliber Spencer carbine and its shells, the regulation Army gun at the time. That's what the soldiers were carrying when they showed up at the Silver King according to Jack Frazer. Those guns give the only clue. That's why I've been running these things down for months. I've got dope here that most people don't know exists," I added, tapping the notebook open on my lap.

"So we look for fired .52 caliber Spencer shells in miles square of this kind of country," Vall said sarcastically.

"You need imagination," I retorted. "Just suppose you're going up that trail where Forest ran out of tracks to follow between Needle and East Boulder Canyons. You got a rifle in your hands, and a deer jumps up. What do you do?"

"Shoot at it," Vall said. "Who wouldn't?"

"Exactly," I agreed. "Then you lever a new cartridge into the chamber and start after the deer for another shot. Then right there the fired shell is ejected on the trail or very close to it. That is where it should still be lying!"

"Oh! You mean the trail between canyons," Vall exclaimed, his eyes glittering suddenly.

"Furthermore," I said. "If a deer runs, you start in the same direction. And there's the ejected shell falling to one side or the other to show which way you went—the way the vein is!"

"By god! That would do it!" exclaimed Vall excitedly now. "If we can find that shell . . ."

And with daylight we were on our way after it, following the old trail again into East Boulder Canyon. There, at first, the trail had been built up flat with rocks and almost wide enough for a wagon, with hundreds of feet of it as perfect as the day it had been made. Further along it vanished completely or narrowed down to a mere path almost lost beneath thickets of catclaw or mesquite. We followed it for almost two miles up East Boulder Canyon until Weaver's Needle, dead ahead, grew to such a gigantic size that the very mass of it towering over us could almost be felt. Then the trail swung across canyon and headed up a shallow arroyo.

"We go to work here," I said. "Somewhere before those soldiers got over to Needle Canyon beyond they jumped that deer."

"This don't look so easy now," Vall observed. "Suppose that shell is under some of this brush?"

"I have that figured out too," I said. "The shell would be a reddish, coppery color. So I'll use a photographic filter on my fieldglasses that'll pass the reddish of the shell but blank out the ground and the vegetation. The shell will stick up like a sore thumb. You just go ahead with a stick and push the brush back to give me a clear view."

We started out that way, taking the south side of the trail toward Weaver's Needle, turning over every large rock, looking under every bush and cactus patch. Occasionally we stopped long enough for a cigarette or sip of water. And then I followed after Vall again with fieldglasses glued to my eyes until they ached. It took us just five hours to get over that scant mile. But still we hadn't seen the shell.

"Maybe they ran out a ways before they pumped a fresh cartridge into the gun," said Vall doubtfully.

"Anything's possible," I replied, tired and a little doubtful myself now. "The only thing I'm going on is that I wouldn't take after a deer with a fired shell in **my** rifle chamber."

We ate a can of corned beef apiece for lunch in the scanty shade of a mesquite. But it was like sitting in an oven, with the air hot and still, with every rock reflecting sun-gathered heat. Then we started back but working the north side of the trail this time.

It didn't seem as though the sunglare could become any more fierce. But by the middle of the afternoon it was burning with a fiery intensity. And the sweat kept running down into my eyes and onto the glasses until I had to stop every few minutes to wipe them off. Then about three hours from Needle Canyon my heart suddenly jumped into my throat. For I was looking at the end of a shell sticking up in some dirt right beside Vall's foot as he bent over to push a bunch of bear grass aside. It looked even plainer than I had pictured it in my imagination.

"Hold it!" I yelled, the heat and sunglare forgotten instantly. "Look by your foot!"

"By god, it was there!" Vall exclaimed unbelievingly, picking it up. And he sat down upon the ground limply like a wet rag.

"It's the right kind, too," I cried, yanking my notebook out of a hip pocket and getting out the clipping.

I sat down too then, about as limply as Vall had, and began thumbing through the notebook. After the heat and constant tension all day the let-down was terrific. Then I found the note I had made of my interview with Jack Frazer.

"A reddish vein about a foot thick, half-way up a black-topped hill," I repeated. "A black-topped hill . . . where the hell is a black-topped hill?"

Both of us looked around a little wildly as though we expected the hill to step up and take a bow. Then I stood up and turned around—and there it was right behind us, about a mile of it in fact, facing the whole north side of the trail. Steep slopes climbed abruptly to tuffa cliffs high above, and sitting on top like a black cap upon a giant head was the dark basalt capping.

"And that's the side the shell was on," I marvelled, still endlessly surprised that it had worked out that way.

"Halfway up a black-topped hill. Then that vein is sure enough there too," Vall exclaimed. His eyes began to shine.

"Think you can find it from here?" I asked.

"For that kind of ore, I could find it in hell," Vall said.

And back in camp that night, there was little talk of anything else until at last we had crawled into our sleeping bags on opposite sides of the campfire. The last thing I remembered were the stars glittering icily in the sky like bright lights along a dangerous road to destiny. Then all at once I was wide awake again with the skin crawling on the back of my neck, with a hard, cold knot seeming to lie heavily upon the pit of my stomach.

The stars had dimmed now in the pale, ghostly glow of a faint, crescent moon. And the fire had burned down to a glowing bed of coals, fanned a dull red by the whispering nightwind. Every now and then a puff of breeze would whip up a whirling shower of sparks which danced away into the gloom like a swarm of fireflies. And in that weird half-light I lay perfectly still, knowing that something was dangerously wrong. An alien noise perhaps or a half-felt presence, I couldn't quite place. Then gradually I began to half-see and half-sense a bulky movement beyond the faint glow of the fire, a shape that seemed to be bending over our packs—over my pack!

Instinctively, without moving in the slightest, without even daring to change the tempo of my breathing, my eyes shuttled to Vall's bedroll. Then I saw that it was flat and empty, that Vall was not there. And in that instant my mind's eye was seeing us once again on the old trail, looking together up at the black-topped mountain. And Vall's harsh voice, vibrant with excitement, was ringing in my ears: "Halfway up a black-topped hill. Then that vein is sure enough there too!" Then it was the night before, and we were sitting around the camp-fire while I was talking: "That's why I've been running down these things for months. I've got dope here that most people don't know exists." And I was tapping the notebook open on my lap.

"The notebook," I thought. "That's what he's after. And that vein that's waiting for the first one to find it. The **first** one to find it."

The thought was like a physical shock, a sudden slap in the face. For there was only one way that Vall could be the **first** one there. And a relentless hand seemed to be gripping my throat all at once, squeezing, squeezing, squeezing so that I could scarcely breathe. It was ages it seemed before I could summon the will to choke back that stark, terrible panic, more ages before I had gained the strength to work my hand toward the revolver under my pillowed coat while I expected any instant to hear the roar of Vall's rifle, while my stomach crawled with the impending shock of the bullet. Then just as he straightened up in the darkness beyond, my hand closed over the hard, cold butt of my gun.

Vall came back toward the fire like a stealthy phantom then, carrying something in each hand. And at last, very faintly through my half-closed eyelids, I saw the metallic sheen of the fireglow upon the naked length of his rifle, and remembered that he had left it leaning against his pack. His rifle! My sudden death!

I rolled over violently, sleeping bag and all, so that on the instant I was flat on my belly and up on an elbow with my revolver levelled. And I felt the trigger going back under my finger. I was even then panic stricken. And I jerked the shot off too hastily at Vall's bulky shadow beyond the fire, heard the crashing echoes. Then I knew somehow that I had missed and savagely rolled back the hammer under my thumb for another, surer shot.

Vall jumped in startled surprise and let both his rifle and my notebook drop. For it was my notebook, I saw as the pages fluttered open. Then instantly he was bending over after the rifle.

"Hold it!" I snarled through the resounding echoes of the shot. And sudden, blind fury replaced the panic in my mind.

I sat up all at once with my gun levelled, and I knew that I wouldn't miss again. And Vall, half-standing and half-bending, froze in his tracks, his dark features working between guilty fear and chagrined indecision. So for a long moment we glared at each other in deadly silence. Then somewhere off upon a remote ridge a coyote howled an answer to the shot, a lonely wail of infinite saddness that came drifting through the gloom like a high, thin whisper on the nightwind. It broke the tension, and at last I was safely guarding Vall with gun in hand until dawn fell finally over the mountains.

"I'm not turning you over to the sheriff," I said. "You'd have a hundred excuses. But you know that I know what you were up to. So you're walking out of these mountains ahead of me. If you ever come back—you'll never leave again."

Later, when I got to First Water myself, I found one of the cowboys there.

"Who was the dark guy," he asked. "He came tearing through here like the devil was after him.

"Maybe it was thunder gods," I said noncommittally. And I knew that I had almost become myself victim of that storied curse.

From the turbulent backwash of time along lonely desert trails the fabulous dreams of yesteryear beckon still with golden lure.

Members of a Storm expedition. Left to right: Hubert D'Autremont testing an unsavory waterhole, Walter Upson, Fred Allen and Gene Holman in cave camp, and Barry Storm near Weaver's Needle.

3. CLUES TO FORTUNE

I have often wished that I had immediately followed up the clue to the soldiers' lost vein after Vall's precipitate departure. But at the time George Snell arrived from Connecticut and Francis Splichal from Kansas too quickly to allow any deviation from the quest for the lost mine trail which Adolph Ruth had followed to his death. Snell had been experimenting for some time in the location with high frequency radio beams of underground metallic objects, and Splichal had a sardonic but brilliant knack for seeing unsuspected relationships between things. I expected considerable help from both of them. So I said nothing at all of the clue except to explain that Vall had been unexpectedly called away, and we began working from my base camp at First Water.

It took weeks of exploration to identify the mineralized region I had marked in upon my topographic map, and many more weeks to learn the lay of the involved East and West Boulder Canyons and the parallel Needle Canyon, all draining down toward the location of my first golden clue miles below. And that mineralized region was our first destination for in it somewhere, I was certain, would be an exact duplicate in reality of the Peralta-mapped **La Sombrera** and accompany hill.

We moved camp to it by easy stages, and at last found that we had to move beyond it into LaBarge Canyon two or three hours away so we could be sure of water and some shade. Then after we had labored for the better part of a week getting our equipment carried over upon our backs jungle style, Abe Reid finally rode through from the Quarter-Circle-U where he had been working.

First, he led us up the hot, cactus-studded slopes of the high mountain between East Boulder and Needle Canyons where he had found the piece of rich ore himself. I knew that he had spent two years hunting its source. And that meant that he had undoubtedly obtained enough first-hand information from his Apache friends to convince him that they had really hidden mines nearby after the Peralta massacre of a near-century ago.

"On this hill?" I asked, thinking that a mountain that was over a mile square according to my topographic map wasn't being very definite.

"Yeh. I knew one of the Indians who helped," Reid explained. "He said medicine men sent a work party of squaws and boys in here to hide the mines so no white man could find them. When I found my piece of gold ore I hit him up to tell me where but he said it was taboo. He was one of the boys and the best he could do was tell me about working on this hill, covering up four mines with half the squaws while the rest hid four more further up canyon. He knew I'd never find them."

"How did he say they covered them?" I asked excitedly, while Snell and Splichal crowded closer to hear his words.

"With caliche-cemented logs over the holes, then dirt and stones to match the ground. They threw ore and tools back in the shafts. Said a loaded packtrain could be driven over them they were that solid."

"What did he say about the other four?" asked Splichal, his thin features taking on the expression of a bloodhound.

"He never saw them himself," Reid explained. "But he said the others told him that they left one open that had just been started high up in some ravine. Another was to the east of the big peak—Weaver's Needle—only the gold there was nuggets in gravel in some tunnels. They laid logs and brush against them. The other two were near a marker to their thunder gods in the canyon."

"A marker?" I echoed. "That's something tangible that can be found."

"That's what I used to think," Reid grinned. "Only it was a big rock set up on a south slope to look like a rampant horse's head. It had something to do with putting a blood curse on the mines. I never could find it. Anyway the canyon runs north-south."

"Then it's straight dope we got eight mines to find instead of the four that the Peralta descendents knew about?" asked Splichal.

"According to the Apaches, you have," Reid agreed.

"They ought to know," put in Snell. "Whatever Pedro found the second time he came back and was massacred wouldn't be known. He couldn't have made maps like he did the first time."

"Sounds logical," Splichal added. "Naturally he'd prospect the country around for more mines later. Who wouldn't?"

And I was thinking with high elation that there might be markers or signs to them also, though I said nothing. For hadn't Adolph Ruth been looking for secret marks!

The next day we followed Reid to the Needle Canyon slope of the same mountain where Ruth's bones had been found in a small arroyo. Reid showed us a cache of the smaller bones which he had found himself later.

The head, he explained, had been discovered first about a half mile away where the killer had hastily buried it in an effort to destroy the only evidence of murder—the bullet hole. And it must have been someone then in the mountains, he pointed out, who had wanted also to make it look like wild animals had destroyed other clues.

"The queer thing is," he said, "that his clothes were shredded and bones scattered around over fifty yards. Wild animals don't even scatter cattle bones over a few feet, just enough to get at the meat."

"Then somebody **overdid** it?" Splichal asked.

"There's proof that the killer overlooked," I explained. "A note in Ruth's own handwriting that the posse found hidden under a flap of his checkbook. A Latin phrase with an interesting addition: **"Veni, vidi, vici**—about 200 feet across from cave.""

"I came, I saw, I conquered," translated Splichal. Then he added excitedly, "Holy smoke! What Ruth actually meant was, 'I came after a mine, I saw a mine, I found a mine! It's about 200 feet from a cave'!"

"He found something alright," said Reid. "I worked later with the cowboys who guided him. One of them told me Ruth knew exactly what landmarks to hunt for. And he was looking for secret markers too."

"Then it checks," Splichal exclaimed. "Reid here couldn't find any mine open. So there must be markers or signs to lead on from the map or Ruth would never have identified the location of a **hidden** mine. His secret memo proves he did that at least."

"And our best bet is to pick up the trail he hit," I added. "A sign-marked trail like the Spaniards used in Mexico, I'll bet."

And in the weeks that followed we tried doing that day after day while the temperature soared up around the 120 degree mark and hardly got below a hundred at night. We kept on crossing and recrossing Needle Canyon for I had decided that the mapped **La Sombrera** had here the greatest similarity to the actual appearance of Weaver's Needle beyond. But we could not quite find a spot where it was an identical likeness in all that welter of tumbled boulders, thickets of mesquite, palo verde and cat-claw. Then one afternoon Snell and Splichal, who had been ranging ahead, came back to report that they had seen nothing but an axe blade sticking in a cactus.

"An axe blade," I almost yelled. "And did you think the thunder gods stuck it there? I want to personally see everything that isn't exactly natural. Take me to it."

I went back up canyon with them to where a lone, huge saguaro stood upon the end of a rocky ridge jutting into the canyon. From the canyon bottom the cactus stood up in bold, spiny outline against the sky as though it had purposely been planted there for just that reason. And it did look like an axe head alright. Then as I moved around another came into view.

"Axe head, hell!" I yelped excitedly. "It's a marker! Made to be skylined for anyone traveling up-canyon."

And we all scrambled up the slope in a wild rush at the cactus. Then I saw that what were sticking out were stones which someone had inserted there purposely. Two of them.

"That ain't all," Snell cried. "Here's holes for more."

I stuck my finger into one that was over two inches deep, and scabbed over like it had been made generations ago. And my fingernail rasped on something rough that wasn't cactus fiber at all. Instead, it was the broken-off end of another stone that had once been embedded that deeply in the cactus.

"Wow!" I exclaimed. "This is plenty old enough for Spanish times."

Then I noticed that the missing stones—there were holes for two—were so set opposite the two still sticking in the cactus that they had been apparently used to mark two straight lines —to what? I tried my compass immediately but those lines lacked a degree or two of exactly checking by either magnetic north or true north. And wouldn't surveyed lines—if that's what they were—be exact. But wouldn't they also have been laid out by compass nearly a century ago?

Excitedly I got out my notebook and looked up the magnetic declinations back through several decades of records that I had copied from Geodetic Survey data. And I had it! I simply turned the declination dial of my compass back to the 12 degrees, 58 minutes east of north that had been magnetic north during the year 1847—and the stone pointers fell into exact compass alignment east and west and southeast-northwest.

"Holy smoke!" exclaimed Splichal. "Then they were put here at the time of the Peraltas!"

"And we've hit Ruth's secret trail, sure as hell!" I added.

And bright and early the next morning we were back there again, looking for the two missing stone. We found them finally at the base of the cactus where they had fallen, after trying most of the loose rocks of similar size lying around. For the missing pieces matched both the cactus holes and broken end to broken end the pieces still embedded.

Had Ruth said that he was looking for such a marker? Most certainly this was proof that the trail he had followed to a hidden mine and sudden death was marked in some fashion. And if it had been done here by Pedro Peralta then why not again when massacre had impended later—a secret trail to the four additional mines which Apaches had found elsewhere and to a fabulous golden treasure in gold from those mines which Pedro must have hidden nearby? A secret treasure trail of which there was no record beyond the mute bones of unlucky miners!

Exultantly then, I knew, both that proof and the kind of markings would be displayed upon this marked trail if that's what we had stumbled upon! But for the life of me I couldn't see what relationship lay between the Peralta map and this marker.

"Suppose it had been made later," said Splichal," when Pedro found out he had to leave his mines. Suppose he made it here on purpose because he could hardly fail to see it the way it's skylined, and only he knew that it would be in **this** canyon."

"It must be a secret key then," observed Snell. "But it's damn hard to figure out what somebody was thinking a century ago. Why this canyon?"

"Wait," I exclaimed. "That's the question I was trying to figure out. Suppose he had made his map from here to start with. That map would locate this canyon. How add a secret marker to be used along with the map which he already had? It wouldn't be by putting that marker on the spot the map would locate, would it?"

And in haste I got out my map copy and climbed up to the marker again, trying to see it reconstructed as though for the first time. Then right from beside it all at once Weaver's Needle upon the horizon beyond jumped to life in an identical mapped outline. So this was the spot from which the peak had been copied. Then where was the hill to one side that had also been mapped? And as suddenly to the northwest was that mapped mountain in all its topographic detail, literally lifting itself up in full size from the map. Just that one instant while I was recognizing it was one of the most singular thrills I have ever experienced.

I let out a yell instantly, and Splichal and Snell jumped up to crowd around me. But all I could do at first was to mutely point from the map to the mountain which it outlined. And with shaking fingers I sighted my compass—still set for the year 1847—at the top. It was exactly northwest. Proof again of an 1847 compass survey.

"That's the way any marked trail is going," I said finally finding my voice. "Else why should Pedro have mapped it?"

I sent Splichal out ahead a hundred yards or so toward the top up a three-quarters mile long steep slope and signalled him into line by compass. Then I started Snell out toward him to follow the same line, searching for another marker. And I came behind Snell. Thus we went hand over hand as it were up to the top, finding along the way an ancient trail worn inches deep in solid rock but now overhung with catclaw and prickly pear to prove that it hadn't been used in decades. Then at last from the top I could look back and see that the trail was perfectly aligned from the key marker in Needle Canyon far below.

I was sure now that this hill was the focal point of the Peralta map—the same black-topped mountain, I saw, on the south side of which I had found the shell clue, on the north side of which Reid had found his piece of ore, on the eastern side of which Ruth's remains had been found, and on top of which Apaches said they had hidden four mines, just too many coincidences in the same location to be really coincidence! And I dispatched a letter to Erwin Ruth telling him about the marker and ancient trail and the deductions I was making from the fact that the Peralta-mapped mountain was a recognizable reality at last. Then during the latter part of July I received an exciting answer in which Erwin Ruth said: "The information concerning my father's (Adolph Ruth's) account of the Peralta mines as described is correct to the best of my knowledge of the subject. I remember father stating that he knew which canyon to travel from **the marker.**"

And this more than ever convinced me that Ruth had been able to identify a hidden mine location upon that same black-topped mountain by secret signs, that he had had good reason for writing the hidden memo which had been found in his checkbook. Most important of all we were actually upon the same trail!

The logic of that was unshakable, even Splichal had to admit. So back we went to work in a search for signs or markers. And I sent Snell ranging ahead with his radio locator, the latest if then still unperfected prospecting tool based upon the fact that a directed beam of high frequency radio waves would be reflected back from any metal or metallic ore underground. Splichal and I followed after, poking under patches of prickly pear and cholla, circling every boulder and ledge of rocks to look upon all sides, always sweating in the hot summer sun. It was like working on top of a griddle except that the fire was everywhere.

Often Snell found low-grade mineralizations which assayed some gold and silver content though at last it became evident that his instrument was not powerful enough to penetrate more than four or five feet underground. Then early one afternoon in mid-August when I had just about given up hope of finding anything further, Snell suddenly set his radio balance down, picked some half-buried object out of the ground and let out a yell.

"A horseshoe!"

But it turned out to be a muleshoe instead, rusted and badly worn, with the nails twisted where it had been kicked off against a rock. Excitedly I recognized its peculiar shape, the ends flaring out in a hand-made pattern used to this day in the back country of Mexico.

"That's it!" I cried. "The one thing I wanted to see with my own eyes—proof that a mule **shod in Mexico** was brought up here! Then it was Spanish signs that Ruth saw. They must be here somewhere."

And that was why I recorded the Mother Lode Mining Claims on the Peralta-mapped mountain. The Peraltas must have used the same kind of signs which had led to the refinding of many abandoned mines up and down the length of the Spanish-held Americas. But if the purpose of the Peralta map was to locate this mountain, or had been originally, and that northwest pointer of the key marker had been added later when massacre impended to point more particularly to the top where we were working then wouldn't the direction line itself be a device to more memory-refreshing clues?   Even to signs?

I thought it was a valid inspiration and I went over to the cliff edge to look down toward the key marker far below.   Then I got out my fieldglasses and compass and gradually jogged myself around to stand directly in line, meaning to see where it might extend on top of the mountain. And I practically stepped upon the Spanish word **"ORO"**—**gold!**—cut into black basalt rock on the very edge.

I was not merely surprised.   I was so startled that I almost stepped off the cliff.   It was a perfect hiding place for signs, and we had been within feet of them without knowing it   I let out a yell.   And while Snell and Splichal came running over all excited expectancy at once, I squatted down still not believing my eyes.   For other signs became visible too near the word, a dotted sunburst which means "a mine is below," and over it a fifty vara mark.   Then separately on another rock a crawling snake which is supposed to point out a trail to treasure or mines.

No wonder the compass lines indicated by the key marker had been so accurately aligned.   The northwest line at least pointed with precision directly through the word, **oro,** and could only have been laid out that way in 1847 for Pedro would have known nothing of earth currents and magnetic declinations.   To him a direction would have been the magnetic one shown by his compass, and this northwest one was so obvious, once the mapped mountain had been identified from the key marker location, that Ruth must have followed it and had somehow identified the site of a hidden mine from these signs and the information upon his original Peralta map. But if the northwest pointer of the key marker had pointed out these signs, I thought exultantly, the other tree pointers would undoubtedly have a similar purpose.

Then Splichal was leaning over the edge of the cliff, looking at something a few feet below.

"More signs!" he exclaimed excitedly, and went down on the huge chunks of basalt which had fallen away to make ledges.

I followed after and found myself staring straight at a cross cut into rock and beside it what appeared to be an involved map. And to one side was a plain sunburst which says, "mines are nearby!" We all excitedly scattered out looking for more but we had already found them all. Then I climbed back on top after my camera, photographed the signs, and sat down to figure them out. It looked to me like a complete set embodying explicit instructions with a detailed map. But the map had no meaning, and was probably some sort of secret key. Splichal and Snell both thought so too for together the signs said:

"Mines are nearby on mapped treasure trail—follow the treasure trail to gold in mines below fifty varas."

We tried doing that for the better part of a month. But fifty varas merely put us down the slope below the cliff. And without Snell's locator to reach far beyond its depth range to find the ore upon which the Peralta miners had left off work or the metal tools which the Indians had thrown back into the shafts, we were effectively blocked—unless I thought it possible to dig up acres of solid rock, a solution beyond my financial means at the time, and a considerable gamble since we could find no interpretation for the map. Finally, even I had to admit that the map itself must have had some simple enough key of its own, some relationship to the surrounding topography which would be instantly obvious to its maker and probably was to Ruth with his first-hand Peralta information but which escaped us as effectively as though there had been no signs at all. And that was more good luck than bad else Ruth's murderer would long since have found the mine site that Ruth had identified.

But commonsense counseled caution, and after the Vall episode I had decided that the wisest policy was simply not to allow any of my helpers to obtain enough information to get anywhere ahead of me along the treasure trails I was following, human nature being what it is. So that fall I sent Snell and Splichal home and set up the little hidden camp in the mountains from which I often later secretly worked, unknown to even my own expeditionists. That fall, too, as I did some more photography and made notes on the ground of as much of the story as I had verified, I became aware for the first time that I was being trailed by an expert mountain man who must have been intimately familiar with every twist and turn in that wild region to so continually elude me. For there were his distinctively small footprints caught in several soft places I had purposely scratched along the trails and beside them. I didn't know that he had probably been watching us work all summer, and would shortly prove it by attempting murder later, that it was undoubtedly Ruth's slayer himself.

In fact, I did too much talking to reporters when I finally left the mountains. And the expedition which I organized in Los Angeles this time was much too well publicized over the entire West by a full page newspaper story, repeated conclusions which must have been highly disturbing to Ruth's murderer, and left the idea that I had found enough evidence to make my first lost mine discovery immediately upon my return to the Supersitions. And other stories of which I didn't learn until it was too late to head them off painted me as a two-gun detective hot upon a murderer's trail, hardly a truthful portrait.

The wild region dominated by Weaver's Needle and beginning with East Boulder Canyon below in which Barry Storm found his first lost mines clues and then discovered from (inset) a secret camp that he was being trailed by a killer.

Bluff Springs Mountain (on left) at Needle Canyon junction marks region in which many lost mine clues were found including beyond the first Peralta mine to be discovered. Left to right are (short arrows) charcoal pit site, Dutchman's campsite and Ruth's remains location; (insets) .45-90 Sharpes rifle shell, pieces of bonanza ore, etc., identifying Dutchman's camp, obsolete square nails from Wiser cache, refound Peralta mine with Burbridge, Peralta key maker, Spanish miner's signs.

4. HIDDEN SPANISH GOLD

I had chosen four this time, Engineer Hubert D'Autremont of Hollywood, jolly Fred Allen of London, England, trailwise Gene Holman of Wisconsin and enigmatic Walt Upson of Los Angeles who had spent much time along Mexican treasure trails. And we set up a base camp on the northern side of the Superstitions miles up LaBarge Canyon in a comfortable cave under overhanging cliffs with a secondary camp seven miles further above at the junction of Needle and Boulder Canyons.

We went to work first from the base camp, panning and prospecting for mineralization. For The Dutchman had said that there were three red hills just north of the region in which his fabulous mine lay hidden. If that were true it meant another but right angle mineralized strata running north-south to cross that trending east-west from Goldfield, an excellent geological site for mines to further localize my hidden mine area since considerable iron content would be necessary to color the rock red. Too, I wanted to find some identifiable evidence for The Dutchman's presence in the region, for just as Adolph Ruth's trail had led to the area of the Peralta-mapped mountain where Pedro had found his first four mines so would The Dutchman's trail lead to the area of other mines which Pedro had discovered upon his return but of which there was no record except among the Apaches who had hidden them. Most imporant, even the Apaches would not know where Pedro had hidden a treasure in already-mined gold when massacre impended. And, I thought, he must have left signs to it also just as he had added signs and the key marker to go along with his original map in the region of his first-found mines. Those additional signs, I was sure, would be near his campsite. For wasn't that there he would have normally planned to return when danger was over?

Then within a space of weeks we made two exciting discoveries, that we could pan out a few "colors" of gold along a multicolored ridge separating Boulder and LaBarge Canyons a short ways above their junction and which trended north-south to ward my involved Needle Canyon area above, and that we were being continually followed everywhere we went. Followed by someone wearing unusually small shoes—the same tracks which I had trapped months before!

We went on with our prospecting though now we carried arms constantly. We panned for gold in a fan-shaped pattern, taking the main canyons as the lower point of a V and the tributary arroyos running up to either side as the upper lines to be eliminated one by one. Thus we followed the multi-colored ridge for nearly a mile where it stood up in bold, ragged outline for hundreds of feet, sometimes scarlet, purplish or yellow from oxidizing minerals. Then the tuffa cliffs closed again over the strata, towering far over it in weather-worn crags. But we had its trend accurately laid out and moved up to the secondary camp to pick it up again. And there were those singularly small tracks once more, fresh from the night before!

After that we lost a lot of sleep, trying to catch a glimpse of our unwanted phantom. Some of us would sit around the campfire for decoys while others hid out in the rocks and brush. Once we though we had him but the crashing of something through the undergrowth turned out to be a cougar dragging off a calf, and we left it hastily alone.

Then the rains came, the usual January rainy season condensed into a week or two. And the upper camp was entirely unsheltered. We slept out in the rain in wet sleeping bags laid upon the wetter ground between two huge bonfires, when we could sleep at all. For the thunder was a crashing cannonade that rumbled on and on incessantly in violent crescendo, shaking the very ground, vibrating the air as though every crag in the Superstitions were tumbling down about our ears at once. And lightning came in sudden, livid sheets of flame, washing up brilliant etchings from the inky blackness of night, of swaying saguaros, wind-lashed trees and sheer cliffs over which lowering clouds rolled. We cooked in the rain, ate in the rain, worked in the rain and damned the rain. But that rain proved to be a rare bit of good fortune, for only treasure hunters would be abroad in such weather.

We not only picked up the reddish strata again exactly upon my charted line and hardly a half mile north of the Needle Canyon region I had already explored, but it came up in the form of three low hills! Then the very next day we found a charcoal pit a short distance away at the foot of Bluff Springs Mountain, a perfect oblong about three feet by five. The rains had sunk its filling of surface dirt in enough below the surface of the ground so that D'Autremont, who spotted it first, yelled that he had found a covered mine. In fact that is what we all thought at first glance as we went excitedly to work upon the sunken outline which looked exactly like a covered shaft was caving in. But after we had dug the dirt out we found a solid three foot layer of charcoal and ashes.

"Hell," Upson exclaimed disgustedly. "It's a Mexican miner's charcoal pit. They use them like a forge for working drill steel."

"Then this is proof that Mexican miners worked around here somewhere," I said. And I thought I had found the Peralta camp.

I looked around excitedly and saw that the flat on which we stood rose up on the south almost immediately into the cliffs of Bluff Springs Mountain which separated Needle and LaBarge Canyons just as the Peralta-mapped mountain separated Needle and East Boulder Canyons but west instead of east. It would be an ideal camping place for anyone working in the vicinity of any of the three canyons nearby.

The next day we returned and spread out across the flat searching in detail for any evidences of an ancient camp—the Peralta camp near which I was sure I would find the start of another sign-marked trail to hidden treasure and unrecorded mines though I kept the intriguing idea to myself lest word of it somehow get out through one of my helpers when their work was done. Then D'Autremont, who was always poking ahead, again made the first find, an obsolete style goldpan almost entirely buried under a palo verde upon the Needle Canyon side of the flat. I helped him work it loose and saw that the rim had been pierced all around by nailholes as though the pan had once been nailed to a frame for washing out gold from hand-mortared rock. And the nailholes were square!

I called excitedly for a shovel myself and began tearing up the ground. Then soon I had located the ashes of a campfire long since silted over, and in the ashes a dozen or so of the obsolete nails to match the square holes. Then nearby a .45-90 Sharpes rifle shell—from the identical type gun The Dutchman had always carried! And the square iron nails had gone out of common use in the 1870's!

"Sure as hell, we've got The Dutchman's camp!" I exclaimed exultantly. "And that makes Needle Canyon the one below his mine!"

For even without the nails as a definite dater I would have seen the connection. The north-south canyon bounded on the north by the three red hills. The cache of Wiser's equipment which, I had learned, had been found by Roy Bradford a short distance away in that same canyon. And in that canyon The Dutchman had told his friend, Reinhart Petrasch, was somewhere the key, a natural stone face, pointing upward toward his mine. But it was trail that would have to await a later expedition.

"This is more than I expected here, men," I exclaimed gleefully. "But I still have to find the Peralta camp that should have been here too but isn't. The only other possible place would be further up LaBarge Canyon where there is permanent water." And I wondered why I hadn't thought of as simple a thing as that before.

The condensed rainy season had helped us there also, for the heavy runoff had removed the surface accumulations of decades to give everything a new, fresh appearance which it hadn't had the summer before. And at last, about a half mile above where I had camped, we began finding occasional pieces of charcoal and bits of burned wood, then finally huge mounds of ashes now laid bare and scattered over a good half acre where the canyon widened out. In one of those ash piles we found a piece of a broken spur with huge rowel, as unmistakable Spanish-Mexican as though a conquistadore had just discarded it there.

Jubilantly, I knew this was it, the Peralta campsite. And I hoped that I was the only living person who had guessed the exciting possibility of the presence of another sign-marked treasure trail beginning—here! So I told Upson that I expected to find definite identification in the form of the miner's signs he had often seen himself in Mexico, and disbanded the rest of the expedition which had done its work well. And then again the small, mysterious footprints of our unknown follower—my follower!—appeared again everywhere we went.

The weather had cleared off now with mid-February to make our daily hike up from the Needle Canyon camp a pleasure. And every day we worked out a little further from the ancient campsite, inspecting every tree, saguaro and boulder for signs. It took just two weeks to widen our circle to a quarter mile around. Then one morning I came upon a large black rock with a square face about eight feet high and twelve feet long on which had been cut in profusion hieroglyphics such as cliff-dwellers had made ages ago. But over these and penetrating much deeper into the rock surface were newer signs, some of them instantly recognizable as Spanish miner's symbols.

I called Upson over with an excited shout and together we examined the rock, agreed that this definitely established the camp as of Spanish-Mexican origin, and that the Peraltas—if it had been they—appeared to have instructed a miner to travel thus and so in the region of the recognizable Weaver's Needle by some key which was not readily apparent. For there was a crude drawing of a bearded Spanish miner with ore sack on back and candles in hat facing toward the outline of Weaver's Needle and a hill beyond which had been sketched in detailed outline, many hills represented by circles, a treasure trail cross and some tunnel signs. And what would a miner travel toward except ore!

I got out my topographic map to see if there was a recognizable relationship between the obvious Weaver's Needle and the other detailed hill, discovered exultantly that it matched in contour shape and exact position north the Peralta-mapped mountain, that the other circles were accurately placed to represent other nearby peaks. The whole thing seemed to be a master map of the region drawn almost to an exact scale with startling accuracy. But there were other marks which neither Upson nor I recognized as having any definite meaning. And we finally decided that Pedro Peralta—for it must have been he who had contoured the mountain which he had mapped— had added secret signs of his own and would have been the only one to know what they indicated.

By this time our grub supply was almost gone so we returned to the lower camp in LaBarge Canyon to rest up a few days before leaving the mountains, Upson to go on a mining job in Mexico to which he was committed and I to do some more writing. And there in the base camp with a full moon flood-lighting the night, silhuetting the ragged cliffs far above, outlining the grotesque saguaros upon the slopes and the delicate tracery of willow branches in the canyon, we decided to move outside of our cave. Then my mysterious follower struck as though he had been patiently awaiting such a chance to stop my explorations.

The time was about 10:30 one night after we had moved our sleeping bags across canyon to the base of a sheer cliff where a sandy patch in the canyon bed made a natural mattress. We had a campfire going there and were lying around it speculating on the hidden signs we had found. Upson had laid his gun belt aside. But fortunately I was still wearing mine.

Suddenly, without the slightest warning, I heard the whine of a high-power rifle bullet zinging like an angry hornet toward me. A mere fraction of a second it must have been while I was recognizing the sound for what it was, while the skin bunched on the back of my neck. Then the bullet plopped into the ground beside me, throwing up a spray of sand. And the crasing echoes of the shot roared out from up-canyon, resounded in a snarling undertone from cliff to cliff.

We were both stunned by surprise. And in that brief space I was already automatically thinking how impossible it would be to shoot accurately in the moonlight with a revolver, was deciding that the only alternative was an answering barrage to disconcert our attacker before he got in another, surer shot. Then Upson was rolling over out of the firelight, was scrambling on hands and knees after his gun.

I dived in the opposite direction for the shelter of a boulder, my gun already out, and started shooting instantly toward the rifle's report, toward a clump of trees and bushes a hundred yards up-canyon. And I felt a vast satisfaction in the vivid, orange flashes of my gunflame spearing out toward that ambuscade, knew that my bullets were crashing into it headlong. I yelled to Upson through the thunderous noise, to fan out to one side and start a crossfire. Then my gun clicked empty and Upson was shooting to cover me while I reloaded and dodged ahead from boulder to tree trunk, flopped down upon my belly thus hoping to get a glimpse of the riflemen skylined against the moonlight. Upson emptied his gun, and I started shooting again. And in the lull afterwards while the crashing reports were filling the canyon to the brim, while Upson moved up to me, I heard a faint, metallic clank as though of gun barrel against stone, a hasty scrambling of footsteps in gravel.

In the sudden silence we waited together, squatting in the moon-dappled shadows and reloading in frantic haste. Then we moved cautiously ahead with guns levelled, worked on up to the trees which stood at the junction of LaBarge and Boulder Canyons, heard faintly from beyond the frantic crashing of someone through the bushes.

The next morning I went over the tracks carefully, read from the trail that the same phantom with the small feet had come down LaBarge Canyon to the bend from which he could command our camp, had waited there in premeditated readiness for murder. For under the trees he could stand completely hidden by shadows and at the same time hold his rifle barrel in a moonbeam to light his sights. So it must have been someone **living** in the Superstitions all along who had decided at last that I was becoming too lucky or dangerous in finding for myself the clues to hidden mines which my deadly shadow wanted. I should have guessed then who it was. But I didn't until after my next expedition that fall which resulted in discovery at last of the stone face told of by The Dutchman, the Apache secret marker and more Peralta evidence in upper Needle Canyon, enough verification at last to decide me to stay alone afterwards to write my booklet, "TRAIL OF THE LOST DUTCHMAN," while trying to induce my phantom to attempt murder again under circumstances where I might discover his identity.

For this time I was using the new camp in upper LaBarge Canyon which my expedition had constructed, hoping thus, after I had disbanded the expedition, to lure him into the open. Once identified, I wanted to hold the threat of an attempted murder charge over him to force him to tell me what he knew about the Ruth murder. And, as I had figured, he appeared again within days after I was alone, appeared one night about 1:00 a. m.

I awoke suddenly then out of a sound sleep to find myself

sitting bolt upright in the darkness of my tent with the strange, crawling feeling that another presence was near, that the gravest danger threatened. Immediately I had my gun in one hand and flashlight in the other from under my pillow, threw back the blankets and swung my feet to the ground. Then the cot creaked with startling loudness and I heard outside the sudden breaking of brush as something fled from within a few feet. But by the time I had fumbled my feet into shoes and had rushed outside that something was crashing away through the undergrowth down-canyon beyond range of my flashlight, something human for no animal would be that clumsy. I fired one hasty shot after it, then looked for tracks after a time. And they were the same small footprints, had approached to within a few feet of my tent.

Again, a week later, when I was standing out in front one morning, a rifleshot sounded from the cliffs above and a bullet zinged past dangerously close to drill a neat hole in the tent. And then one mid-afternoon soon after, when some half-heard unnatural noise brought me away from my writing, I ducked outside just in time to see a slight motion in a clump of bushes below camp. I yanked out my gun and started that way on the run, thinking that at last I had my unwelcome follower dead to rights. I never did catch sight of him. Instead, I found where he had been hiding, found again those unusually small footprints.

This time I backtracked them for a considerable distance and discovered that instead of following the trail my phantom was walking to one side where his tracks would not show. Thus he had been coming and going, perhaps awaiting a sure shot at me, without leaving anything to attract my attention to his presence. It wasn't until then that I remembered that same trick which I had observed once before from my secret camp in upper East Boulder Cayon, and something clicked into place in my mind. For I was remembering too that Adolph Ruth had worn size six shoes, that those shoes had never been found though fresh tracks made by them had been seen many months after Ruth had died, that I had seen a man in the region making the same size tracks. And there wouldn't be many feet which could fit into Ruth's shoes! Small feet, small man! And if he hadn't had an actual part in the Ruth murder then why the shots at me **only after** I had discovered clues to lost mines? Why the continual surveailance so long as I was in the involved region even when I was writing rather than mine hunting? So back at my typewriter I tried to expose him in the pamphlet. But my publisher had the too pointed remarks deleted though somehow my amazingly accurate forecast of the description and almost exact location of the "gold nuggets in gravel" mine, which I was to actually discover, was allowed to stand unverified.

The pamphlet was published February 1939. And when Harry Hansen raved in the New York World-Telegram, "Makes me want to buy a spade and a pair of boots," and Paul Jordon-Smith added in the Los Angeles Times, "Alluring little book that may lead to somebody's fortune!" I knew that I was on the track of a real story. But I hadn't yet found a lost mine to prove that story.

I tried again that fall with an expedition from San Diego as recorded in the **San Diego Union** of October 25, 1939 by the headline: "LOST DUTCHMAN MINE HUNTERS WILL TRY OUT RADIO LOCATOR." For I had just investigated the latest developments in such electronic devices, had found that Dr. Gerhard Fisher of radio compass homing beam fame had applied the principles of electro-magnetic induction to his patented Metalloscope. So if it seems incredible that I should have taken my own published advice and found the lost mine whose location I had foretold, I must here credit the Metalloscope which made it possible to trace the conglomerate ore which my expeditionists found east of Weaver's Needle to check exactly with the "gold nuggets in gravel mine" over tunnels of which Apaches had laid logs and brush a near-century ago. But the Apaches did not know that those tunnel locations—if I were right in my deductions—had long since been disclosed by Pedro Peralta upon his master map!

In fact, my original plan, after my expedition had completed its prospecting work to localize the matching type of drift ore that fall, had been simply to backtrack that ore to the location indicated by the tunnel signs and then start blasting up and down the nearby cliff with thrown dynamite bombs to blow the tunnel coverings in. But instead, as I explored alone from my hidden camp again during February 1940, I came upon the ruins of a breastworks, an ancient defense against Indian attack, in the same area. And with this lucky localizing clue, I saw that very same afternoon the man-made tunnels in the small, characteristically Spanish fashion, some gaping open and others partially covered by fallen rubble to show how the cliff face had crumbled away at last to expose them. It must have been the heavy January rainy season which had caused it for none of us had seen a thing, except the occasional pieces of conglomerate ore, the fall before to indicate the presence of those tunnels.

But it was a lost mine, a Spanish mine! Proof that the Peralta legends were not legends but golden history! Proof that Apaches had hidden, as they had told Reid, eight mines instead of the four known to Peralta descendants. Proof that there were in the weird Superstitions two different treasure trails signed-marked to mines—and undoubtedly now the fabulous treasure trove in already mined gold from nearly a year's production from those mines! And I was just barely in time!

Three prospectors, working from the south side of the mountains, I later found out, stumbled upon my backtrail, and themselves found the tunnels a short while later. Then at the same time two members of my second 1938 expedition also working unknown to me from the same area and apparently tracking the prospectors, filed prior mining claims ahead of the prospectors by a nose. A notorious gunman appeared suddenly, one of the prospectors vanished under mysterious circumstances and the others fled, and the gunman himself filed claims only to be arrested by the sheriff. And as suddenly a mining engineer from another part of the state moved in with a veritable army upon the gunman's claims, my sanguine former expeditionists were forced out at gunpoint, and mining began behind armed patrols. There was no longer any secret to this proof for both my story and the sign-marked treasure trail which I left this lost mine to follow. And on March 26, 1940 the news story which I verified for the United Press proclaimed: "LOST SPANISH GOLD MINE FOUND! SUPERSTITION GOLD MINE DISCOVERED!"

My own first inspection of those ancient tunnels, the reason why I filed no claims myself, had satisfied me that while there were possibly many thousands of dollars worth of ore left—and it is said that the mining company which promptly cleaned them out behind armed guards shipped $87,000 worth to the smelter! —the pioneer Peralta miners had already gotten the best of it by the time massacre had impended a near-century ago. And taken from a mine location recorded only upon the master map in LaBarge Canyon! But only I knew now that the golden production from that mine—plus that from seven more "lost" by the Peralta massacre!—had never left the Superstitions!

It is still there where Pedro Peralta buried it, this fabulous horde of thunder gods' gold, guarded still by restless Spanish ghosts and an ancient pagan curse. It is still there in that wild frontier land of towering crags, shadowed canyon-chasms and all those turbulent dreams of yesteryear.

Thunder gods' gold is still there—and perhaps one day I'll find it. But now **your** chance is as good as mine!

Barry Storm using the Fisher "M-Scope" electronic locator which helped him find a lost mine in the Superstitions.

Lost mines, like the prospect for new ones, are only found within (A) barren areas intruded by (B) mineralized formations in which (1) veins of comparatively intense richness often appear between (2) footwall and (3) hanging wall to indicate it of different geologic age or rock type a fissure between which the vein filled.
—Courtesy Southwest Pub. Co. from "Practical Prospecting"

5. EPILOGUE

I suspect by now, human nature being what it is, that I, who seemingly don't care a hang about anyone's "history" unless I have found proof for it along some alluring treasure trail, might well be suspected of having thereby discovered far more about the probable locations of more hidden fortunes than I have disclosed. So I hasten to add that I have kept the writer's faith and have held back nothing of importance to the verified legend which I have presented or the fascinating chance of finding the lost mines with which it deals, that I am grinding no axes, have nothing for sale, am not for hire—and that any reader is free to follow the clues which my uncommonly persistent investigation, far more field work than I have herein detailed, a careful sifting of many claims and counterclaims and the "compositing" of many memories has produced. I have ignored only the alleged knowledge of those mercenarily insincere individuals who refuse to spend their own time and money upon the secret clues, exclusive maps and prospecting services they would sell to others. Nor do I claim any originality for the legendary basis of the typical Western treasure tales which I have told.

History, I might point out, is not really history in the accredited sense until its sequence of events has been verified. So, on the contrary, I have often found in achieving this verification that I wrote at considerable variance with generally accepted legend what I have personally seen, heard, experienced and therefrom deduced. And for the personal factors of observation, experience and deduction I most certainly do claim originality—the originality of perceiving and bringing together **in agreement** when I could verify them those many isolated scraps of authentic knowledge often jealously guarded by numerous individuals **in disagreement.**

In fact, I anticipate the disagreement of many with both the story and the data authentifying it which I have presented herein. And to all of them I put this question in advance rebuttal: Have they who claim the knowledge or experience which confounds my own actually put it to the test **inside** the Superstitions? If not, then how do they know whereof they speak? If not, then may I not be pardoned for asking their indulgence? For I have!

So I claim originality in the way that I have verified a thrilling epitomization of romantic frontier history by reconstruction of legendary events, in the way I have focused from scattered scraps of knowledge and evidence those events upon the region of their actual occurrence, thereby discovering that fascinating proof therein which made of mere legend this typical case history, as it were, of Western treasure trove—as complete a case history, that is, as could be obtained without finding **all** of the lost mines involved!

This verification of treasure legend I consider an original and important contribution to the lore of Western America, and one which could hardly be obtained with historical authenticity in ony other way. For all the countless scores of such legends—which perhaps now are not so entirely legendary after all!—to be heard about as every crossroad in every Western state are one with the people there and the land, part of a fascinating heritage. part of our own, of America's real traditions.

Lost gold! Hidden gold! Thunder gods gold! No new vogues are these. But what eternal dreams!

APPENDIX

"The moving finger writes; and having writ,
Moves on; nor all your piety nor wit
Shall lure it back to cancel half a line
Nor all your tears wash out a word of it."

—OMAR KHAYYAM.

1. NOTES OF AUTHENTICITY

1. Early 17th-century chart of Mexico and the American Southwest when California was still thought to be an island—and not without reason. There are among Colorado River Indians tribal traditions of an inland sea. And who in the Southwest has not heard of the ship, loaded with gold, whose spectral spars appear at infrequent intervals from the desert sand dunes near Yuma?

2. "BARRY STORM WILL LEAD SEEKERS FOR LOST ARIZONA ORE," from The Mining Record, October 23, 1941, was one of numerous stories touched off by my most recent search in the Superstitions, interrupted shortly after by the war. Lead paragraphs state: "Barry Storm, Arizona writer-adventurer, who won title of '1941 Model Prospector' at a recent session of the Phoenix Engineers Club for his demonstration of the M-Scope metal locator, ultra-violet ray Mineralight, photographic filters and other modern mineral finding aids, was in Tucson late in November outfitting for a prospecting trip into the Superstition Mountains, scene last year of a "lost" Spanish mine rediscovery and reputed location of the legendary Lost Dutchman Lode." One day I'll return to conclude that unfinished business.

2. "LOST WHEELBARROW MINE RE-DISCOVERED," reported by Associated Press April 16, 1940 from Palouse, Washington, is an excellent example of Western lost mine tradition suddenly verified. I quote: "Ore reportedly running $8,000 a ton Tuesday lifted the Lost Wheelbarrow gold mine out of the legendary class. For years the story of the lost vein had been circulated through the mining country, its fabulous richness half believed and half scorned. Tuesday, however, L. J. Moore, mine manager, announced the vein had been struck after only twenty-two feet of digging and experts said the value of the quartz would run "at least" $8,000 a ton. The story of the lost mine itself—how it was found, abandoned and lost, and found again more than half a century later by a country doctor tramping the hills on vacation—reads like Western fiction. The mine, on what is known as Gold Hill, in the Moscow Mountains north of Potlatch, Idaho—a rugged country—was first discovered according to legend, by a pair of grizzled prospectors in 1883. They found their bonanza in quartz so rich their crude hand mining and milling methods netted them nuggets and dust worth $20,000 (about $35,000 now). Then the legend goes, greed overcame one of the partners. A rifle shot or blow with a pick, it was never known which, ended one life and doubled the fortune of another. Before the remaining partner trudged away the entrance to the tunnel had been blown, covering the crime and leaving only a whiskey-barrel wheelbarrow to mark one of the richest finds in the West. Years later the partner returned but underbrush and time had covered the pot of gold. Last summer, Dr. C. Landis Treischler hit the trail that led to the foot of the rainbow while walking along a faintly indicated mountain path. After staking the claim the doctor and friends unearthed first an ancient wheelbarrow made from a whiskey barrel, then some human bones in the tunnel mouth and an 1875 model rifle. The richness of the vein supports the balance of the legend." In every Western state it has often been so found!

2. "MARVELOUS ORE LIES BURIED NEAR PYRAMID," from the Reno Evening Gazette, November 5, 1941, tells of rich float found by John Durkin near Pyramid Lake, Nevada. I quote: "One square block weighing a ton or more was found, on one side of which was a solid sheet of amalgam two inches or more in thickness. The lowest assay ever taken on any of the float ran 800 ounces of silver, 3 ounces of gold and 35 pounds of quicksilver to the ton, while other samples contained twice the value." I might add that I would have made a deal with deputy sheriff Henry McNamara of Reno, who knew Durkin well, had I not at the same time become involved in tracing ore from the Lost Tonto Trail Copper Lode in Arizona. But now it has become another addition to legend for Durkin meanwhile has died and McNamara at 67 is getting too old for treasure hunting. I quote to Durkin's memory from the California Mining Journal, August, 1942: "John Durkin, one of the most successful prospectors operating in Nevada, died in Reno June 26. He made numerous discoveries and sold several promising properties." And among them an unrecorded and previously unknown Spanish gold mine in Nevada as reported by the Desert Magazine, January, 1941: "Location and survey of the Bunker Hill group of eight claims in rugged country ten miles south of Virginia City have been completed by John Durkin of Reno and B. E. Sweet of Hayward, California. The ground covers what is believed to be the workings of an ancient Mexican mine. Although there is no sign of a road approaching the location, there are 2,000 feet of workings on an inclined plane." Where then is the history which should have recorded these things?

2. "LOST SPANISH MINE FOUND" goes with the story, reported by United Press from Denver, Colorado, February 9, 1940, of how Mandel Torres came upon a weather-beaten piece of hewed timber near the summit of Culebra Peak, and " 'I wondered what timber was doing so far above timber line,' he said. 'I dug and almost fell into the covered-over shaft.' Torres said he explored the shaft—dodging decaying timbers and the dust of centuries—more than 300 feet into the mountainside." Extraordinary? Not at all. From New Mexico Don Pedro Pino reported to the Spanish congress at Cadiz in 1812: "In this province mines have been found closed, some of them with work tools inside, but it is not known at what time they were discovered and worked." Human nature does not change even though tax laws do! For it seems that only a comparatively few who mined fortunes from unknown wilds ever paid their royal fifth to the king of Spain. Reason enough for the traditions of treasure trove known to every Western community!

2. "DUTCH OVEN MINE" headline is from an article by Rexford Bellamy in the Desert Magazine, October, 1941, examining the possibility that Clifford Gillespie's rich strike of $500 a ton gold ore in the Old Woman Mountains south of Danby, California is in reality the long sought abandoned bonanza near which Tom Schofield found a rusting dutch oven full of nuggets in June, 1894, supposedly in the Clipper Mountains to the north. Well a man can mistake his direction! So what then of those uncounted scores of other lost mines known to be in every state west of the Mississippi—and in many states to the east?

2. "OLD SPANISH WORKINGS IN SUPERSTITION MOUNTAINS FOUND IN CLIFF BY PROSPECTORS" is from the Los Angeles Times, March 27, 1940, and details discovery of the Lost Peralta mine which I found, which two of my expeditionists also found as witness their prior claim recordings in Florence, Arizona, and which was found yet again by a party of prospectors at about the same time—before the whole countryside arrived! In my "Trail Of The Lost Dutchman," published February, 1939,

I had over a year previously to this discovery publicly foretold the almost exact location of this "nuggets in gravel" mine. So Paul Jordon-Smith who wrote in the Los Angeles Times, May 14, 1939: ". . . an alluring little book that may lead to somebody's fortune . . ." might have been pardoned in reviewing this sanguine piece of journalism. Imagine my own surprise!

2. "LOST COPPER MINE IN ARIZONA FOUND," from The Mining Record, March 19, 1942, is one of various stories too numerous to list, telling how I matched an ancient packtrail to an equally ancient Arizona legend and found at the junction of both the Lost Tonto Trail Copper Lode. I quote: "Another lost mine legend was reported shattered with discovery by Barry Storm, Arizona writer-adventurer, of a "fabulous" copper lode sought since days of the roaring West when erratic appearance of rich ore reputedly half metal excited pioneer travelers on the old Tonto Trail in the Four Peaks Mountains region over half a century ago." I will add that in my scrapbook I have an ancient claim notice for the Territory of Arizona dated December 23, 1906 and signed by I. E. and W. D. Crabtree whose former pioneer home is now under the waters of Apache Lake just below Tom O'Connell's cabin. They will be delighted to learn that the hole they put down and abandoned up Ash Creek was only a quarter mile from the vein!

2. "CLUE TO LOST ADAMS DIGGINS" are offered in a letter published in The Desert Magazine of May, 1944 by Thomas Childs, who seems to know what he is talking about. Though this may or may not be the same Adams Diggins tradition of the Arizona-New Mexcio border, it is well enough descriptive of traditions which are increasing in even this cynical 20th-Century. I quote: "About 1925 I had a store in Rowood where the highway crew came for provisions. One day one of the crew named Johnston came in and said that the son of the foreman had picked up a man named Adams who was suffering for want of water. Adams had a handkerchief in which he had wrapped about two pounds of gold nuggets which he said he had found northwest of three peaks two or three miles from there. The peaks he mentioned are known by the Indians as Tan Rabia, or High Well. When Adams had recovered from his thirst he appeared at his benefactor's house and offered to take him where he had found the gold, but his offer was not accepted. Later on I saw the foreman's son and had the same story direct from him. He said Adams had returned twice but he still refused to go because he had a good job and didn't know anything about gold. I asked him if he didn't realize that the man was offering to give him more gold than he could earn in 20 years of hard labor. In 1883 I was living in old Gila Bend, when an Indian brought in several very rich pieces of gold specimens, which he said he had found in this same area. Father and myself went out to look for it but failed to locate it from the description the Indian had given us. I tried again in 1927 to find this Adams prospect and did find some very large pieces of placer gold about four miles north of where Adams said his gold came from. Adams claimed he found a white quartz ledge that crossed a small wash and that the gold was all along the wash bed and in the ledge. Adams claimed to have lost his burros. A Mr. Bender who has a cattle ranch nearby told me that he did see the burros also the men but did not know about the gold." And what Westerner cannot verify some such chapter of never-ending, unrecorded history!

3. "LOST SPANISH GOLD MINE FOUND," "SUPERSTITION GOLD MINE DISCOVERED," are various versions as reported nationally by United Press and all major radio networks March 26, 27, and 28, 1940. I quote from the Los Angeles Daily News of March 27, 1940: "The word spread along "Prospector's Row" tonight that an abandoned Spanish gold mine of unbelievable wealth had been found in the heart of the Superstition Mountains in the area in which the fabulously rich Lost Dutchman Mine is believed located. Discovery of the mine, apparently one worked in the early 1800's by Spanish adventurers, was verified here by Barry Storm, writer and adventurer who has spent more than three years in the Superstitions, and Walter Upson, a mining engineer who has just returned from a visit to the newly found workings. "It's not certain that this mine is the Lost Dutchman," Upson said. "But the low passageways, the clumsy timbering and the oxcart trails leave no doubt that it was originally a Spanish mine." The engineer said he had crawled into some of the passageways and found evidence of high producing lode. Storm said the newly discovered workings answered the description of a mine developed by the Spanish adventurer Peralta in the 1840's. "Peralta and his men worked several mines around Weaver's Needle until they were massacred by the Apaches. Until now a lot of people said the story of the Lost Dutchman was all myth and that the Spaniards had never been near the Superstitions, but this should convince them." It did!

4. The Lost Padre Mine to which I refer—there are several traditions of the same name in as many parts of the Spanish Southwest, all traceable to expulsion of the Jesuits from the Spanish Americas during the 1760's when "padres" everywhere buried their mission treasures and covered their mines—is that 30-odd foot hole in the Chocolate Mountains of Southern California which was in the traditional place but which had long since been gutted of a high-grade gold "pocket" from the evidence by the time I had found it. I also have encountered two different men who also successfully traced this legend to its source—too late!

5. R. E. Twitchell in Vol. I of his "Leading Facts Of New Mexico History" reports about the Santa Rita: ". . . Pike in 1807 refers to a copper mine west of the Rio Grande . . . yielding 20,000 mule loads of metal annually . . This must have been the Santa Rita . . . The metal was transported to the City of Mexico by pack mules and wagons . . ." Many early American as well as Spanish maps of this territory which I have seen locate "copper mines" where the Santa Rita is busily producing copper today.

6. I have heard at least a dozen different versions in as many Western states of the traditional Spaniards fleeing toward Mexico with a treasure from an unnamed mine, taking refuge against a cliff from Indian attacks, secreting their "ingots of gold" or "bars of silver" and then getting massacred. Often there are one or two survivors who find that time has covered the end of their rainbow or changed the landmarks of their maps. So very probable in a wilderness infested by hostile savages was an occasional happening of this sort. But it wasn't until 1941 when I ran into a prospector named Reynolds—while I was in the Santa Catalinas chasing the Big Nugget Vein and couldn't do anything about it—that I heard of some tangible proof for one of these legends. Reynolds had found part of a cliff blasted off in Southeastern Arizona, a filled in shaft under it, and in that part of the shaft which he had excavated to date pieces of ancient fuse which he had had a powder company identify as of German manufacture shipped to Mexico during the 1770's. I hope by now that he has dug down

to the "seven jack loads of bullion" which I couldn't get away to find for him with my radionic locator.

7. The exciting facts of Tumacacori are this, that from maps made by Father Eusebio Kino and from the diary kept by his soldier companion, Mange, both the original village and mission of Tumacacori were in 1699 upon the east bank of the Santa Cruz River in southern Arizona. But all evidence of both had vanished long before Americans invaded the country enroute to the California gold rush. Today the mission Tumacacori stands upon the west bank of the river, though as late as 1822 a burial entry by Father Ramon Liberos shows that he had then removed the remains of Fathers Gutierrez and Carillo from the old church to the new. Kino died in 1711, and sometime between this date (Kino's diary gives no evidence of mining) and the expulsion of Jesuits ordered by Carlos the Third, King of Spain in 1767, an unrecorded chapter of mining history occurred to give rise to traditions of the Tumacacori treasure, the Lost Escalante Mine, and the Indian tradition of "The Mine With The Strong Door." This lost chapter of history rightfully belongs with the lost Tumacacori mission though generations of treasure hunters, not knowing about it, have dug many holes about the site of the newer church. But not quite deep enough! In 1921 the present mission building was repaired by the government archaeologist, Frank Pinkley, whose trained eye detected in the right wall about two thirds of the way down the inside of the altar room a single brick which had apparently been placed there at a much later date than the original wall and which this writer believes still is the hiding place of treasure maps relating to the old Tumacacori tradition, though no investigation has been made. In the winter of 1934-35 a complete excavation with a view to renewing the buildings were made by government National Park Service men under direction of Paul Beaubien upon the present Tumacacori site, but no report of the buried treasure they found ever reached the public, though John D. Mitchel, who had used a Fisher radionic locator there, wrote June 14, 1935 to Herbert Sutherland of Mesa: "Some weeks ago while making a trip to the southern part of the state I happened at the Tumacacori Mission and while there saw a large number of men excavating on the east side of the mission where your treasure finding machine indicated to us some months ago that something was buried there. Directly under the spot where we marked a cross and placed a rock on top of it, they found a large adobe smelter and a large amount of gold, silver and copper bullion. By the side of the smelter was found some large pieces of silver bullion, too heavy for us to lift. These pieces are now in the storeroom at the mission. Several smaller smelters were found a short distance east of the large one and under the places marked by us when going over the ground with your radio machine." With such exciting evidence for traditions of Tumacacori treasure at the newer mission, what then might be at the old? And what of the sources of ore which required smelters for its reduction? But most exciting of all, in how many other places in the Spanish-held Americas did the Franciscan fathers, who took over all missions upon the expulsion of the Jesuits, engage in unrecorded mining and in the secret accumulation of treasure troves?

8. For history there is "The Journey Of Coronado, Recorded By Castaneda" by George Parker Winship; "Spanish Explorers In The Southern United States" by Theodore H. Lewis and Frederick W. Hodge; "Spanish Exploration In The Southwest" by Herbert E. Bolton; "Spanish Missions Of The Southwest" by Cleve Hallenbeck, to name a few of the many available. I owe them nothing.

9. For an eyewitness account of Cortes' fantastic adventurers read "The True History Of The Conquest Of Mexico, 'written in the year 1568 by Captain Bernal Diaz Del Castillo, one of the conquerors, translated from the original Spanish by Maurice Keatinge, London, 1800'." There is an American reprint which is not as formidable to read as its long subtitle would indicate.

10. "Apache Gold & Yaqui Silver" by J. Frank Dobie treats in legendary detail the history of the fabulous Tayopa Mine in the wilds of the Sierra Madres. And when C. B. Ruggles so dramatically discovered it after a fantastic $65,000 search which netted some three millions in bullion so one of his men later told me, Dobie rode muleback over those same mountains to cover the story for a 1926 issue of Country Gentleman and see for himself what tradition turned into hard cash looked like. However, there never was found the main cache of 25 million pesetas of bullion which tradition also said was stored beyond a "door of iron bars" set into a mountainside cave.

11. About the Gloria Pan, I quote a letter from engineer H. I. Leuffer sent me from Lluvia de Oro—which means "rain of gold!"—Mexico, dated August 10, 1938. Mr. Leuffer had worked mines for various clients for years in the region—and had spent his spare time trying to locate the Gloria Pan. "The story goes that previous to 1642 from the town of Tubares the early Spaniards worked two very rich mines, the Gloria Pan and Fuego de Barral, neither of which have ever been located. They say there were three mines in the Gloria Pan group: El Peligro, Santa Magdalena and San Jose de Gloria Pan. From these mines many millions of pesetas in gold bullion are stored in the neighborhood. I think the Gloria Pan mine is hidden, and kept that way." For those interested I will add that Tubares is a reality as is the Arroyo de Gloria Pan coming into the Rio de Fuerte just below from the mountain across the river also called Gloria Pan. On the mountain a cave containing skeletons was found, and to this day the hopeful may still decipher the signs there.

12. "Pay Dirt" by Glenn Chesney Quiett, "a panorama of American gold rushes," attempts quite successfully to give in one volume the whole fantastic picture.

13. "A History Of American Mining" by T. A. Rickard will prove interesting as it sketches significant episodes in the ever widening development of American mineral resources.

14. I am indebted to Mrs. J. Lee Lovelace of Chandler, Arizona whose own investigations of the Peraltas, both through diplomatic channels and personally in Mexico, helped considerably my own unraveling of ancient history in such a thorough manner. I held many consultations with her in the summer of 1937 during which she graciously and unselfishly furnished me the results of her own extensive researches.

15. In a letter addressed to me and dated July 24, 1937 Erwin C. Ruth disclosed the source of the Peralta Mine map which caused his father's death in the Superstitions so many years later. Ruth also made available to Dan Jones, Phoenix City Detective who was trying to solve the murder, much similar information.

16. Jack McDaniels some years ago used to cross the Salt River on the Horse Mesa Dam and travel up Alder Creek to his quartz crystal mine near the summit of the Four Peaks. It was on his last trip up Alder Creek that he came upon a ledge of brownish quartz heavily studded with free gold which very probably is alternately exposed and hidden by action of the weather. I am indebted to Abe Reid who hunted for it afterwards and to Tom Collins who saw a piece, for details. I might add that a few miles east in Seven Cottonwoods Canyon a thousand dollars or so in a hatful of ore was found in the same amethystine quartz.

17. In the process of animal evolution one singular fact is outstanding. Always since the dawn of time the inevitable tendency has been for individual units to congregate together and become more complex at the expense of individuality until now we have the phenomenon of vast human groups seeking each other's exploitation by mass military or political force. With such imposition of the mediocre standards of the herd upon the individual the qualities of daring initiative and individual enterprise are forever lost, simply because there remains no personal motive for their development. A prospector, for instance, hardly finds it worthwhile to risk life and limb and gamble his money upon the chance for fortune when he knows that organized human herds will immediately tax or otherwise rob him of the fruits of his labor through sheer weight of political power. Since this is considered—and rightly—nothing but robbery by those who still live by individual creative enterprise at no expense to the herd, such individuals feel morally justified in secreting their fortunes. In late years there have been more treasures consigned to the ground than have been taken out! I would suggest a careful reading of James Harvey Robinson's "Mind In The Making" for a complete understanding of the mental processes involved.

18. Refer to topographic map composed of adjoining sections of the Florence and Roosevelt quadrangles of the U. S. Geological Survey.

19. As photographed August, 1937 from site of the key marker in the presence of George Snell and Francis Splichal.

20. My copy of the Peralta map is a carefully put together composite of those copied from Ruth's original by many local people and of memory-made copies later drawn by Ruth's son. I consider it essentially identical with that carried by Ludi and Jacobs in 1871 and sixty years later by unlucky Ruth since it proved accurate enough to locate the Black-topped Mountain once its function was understood. Ruth's original. I am told by those who saw it, had the top part, probably containing detailed directions which Ruth had memorized and then destroyed, torn off, and across its bottom a notation reading, "Peralta, June 1866," obviously added later. The date in English indicates that it had been so marked by Gonzales to show its source from a Peralta ancestor at the time he had given it to Erwin Ruth.

21. Triangulation from two or more prominent landmarks, which were outlined upon a map as they looked from a common point, was the frontiersman's most common and practical method for locating a region by such cross-bearings focusing upon it. Thus, with this map, it was only necessary to travel from any point reached in the Superstitions around the dominant "La Sombrera" or Weaver's Needle until its shape matched that which had been drawn, and then towards it until the black-topped mountain from a different direction also matched. And one would arrive at the point from which both had been drawn. Probably because of this fact, Pedro Peralta hastily constructed the key marker upon this site when massacre impended to indicate the locations of his miner's signs and other more detailed directions, his original map thus becoming the location key for all no matter how widely scattered.

22. The Dutchman's original map, which he gave to Julia Thomas in a sealed envelope, vaguely located the area a mile or so north of Weaver's Needle in which a natural stone face upon a south slope in a north-south trending canyon pointed upward toward a hidden arroyo in which his mine lay. According to Reinhart Petrasch who attempted himself to use this map in 1882 upon an expedition with Julia Thomas, it was not detailed enough. Later Julia Thomas gave the map to a Richard Holmes who himself accompanied Julia Thomas upon another fruitless search. After the map was thus proved valueless both Thomas and Holmes made and sold many copies. Holmes later claiming that it had been given him personally by The Dutchman along with sample nuggets and many secret deathbed instructions. The truth is, according to Petrasch who was there, that Holmes was then a rank newcomer to Phoenix, and if The Dutchman spoke to him at all it was in the next life, not this. Holmes' son, not knowing the circumstances or his father's flair for promotions, has spent many fruitless years searching himself. Thus does history give birth to legend!

23. Colonel Jack Walker many years later himself disclosed the facts and allowed many of his neighbors—a few of whom made copies—to see Wiser's crudely mapped trail, swinging around Weaver's Needle and apparently ending at the horse's head hill in Needle Canyon. However, when Walker's thoughts sanguinely turned to following that trail, his wife "accidently" destroyed the map during a session of housecleaning. But not before Tom Weeden, Florence newspaper owner saw it and made the investigation that convinced him Walker really had fallen upon an easy trail back to the Lost Dutchman, and tried, in fact to organize a partnership search with Walker for the mine.

24. Wagoner's mapped trail, which originally looked like a fishhook around the Picacho Butte with the shank falling into the canyons' courses, has been modernized to embody recognizable landmarks. In fact, there were at least two of these maps in existence, one of which didn't turn up until many years later with the sequel to Wagoner's story. For Tex Barkley tells, incidently, of a man named Pinkey who had once been one of Wagoner's many grubstakers or "partners" and who showed up at the Quarter-Circle-U Ranch some years ago with a letter and the map signed by Wagoner but dated twenty years before. The contents of the letter indicated that Wagoner (whether as a result of too much wealth or not) had actually ended up in a Tucson hospital within a year or so after he had vanished. He then had sent the map to Pinkey with instructions to meet him near "the board house" (Whitlow's Ranch) for a last trip to the gold. But Wagoner died instead, and Pinkey came at last to the wrong board house—just twenty years too late for his rendezvous with fortune! Of such stuff are treasure hunter's dreams made!

25. My Jenkins' map is a composite of one made for me by Wilma Jenkins in January 1941 and of three made for me by Mrs. Marion Jenkins during April 1939, January 1941 and June 1941. Along with the

last map I signed an agreement with Mrs. Jenkins. acknowledging receipt of the confidential data she had furnished me after Bill's death, and for which "I hereby agree to give Mrs. Marion Jenkins one-third share if located." At the time I had a treasure hunter's deal on with Don Quinn to go after Jenkins' Lost Lode, but at the last minute Quinn's doctor forbade him to engage in anything so strenuous and I, instead, found a gold-bearing vein in the Santa Catalina Mountains which engaged my attention for some time after.

26. All such Spanish miner's signs and the map upon the summit of the southeastern corner of the Peralta-mapped mountain were discovered by me in the presence of George Snell and Francis Splichal, August 25, 1937, and were then photographed. At that time microscopic examination proved, because of long exposure to weathering which had worn individual rock grains to smoothness in the deepest part of the cuts in rock making the signs, that they had been cut a near-century ago.

27. The Peralta "master map," which must have been made along with the key marker in Needle Canyon when massacre impended in 1848, was discovered by myself and Walt Upson, February 12, 1938 above the junction of LaBarge and Charlebois Canyons.

28. By referring to the topographic map it will be seen that due east by the compass according to the declination of 1847-48 from the signs location upon the Peralta-mapped mountain and from the east pointer of the key marker in Needle Canyon is located the space enclosing the former camp and the master map in La Barge Canyon though nearly two miles and Bluff Springs Mountain separates them. This proves the connection between all, with the compass declination disclosing the year that the east-west lines were surveyed by Peralta. There is no doubt that when properly deciphered and interpreted the detailed master map in rock will disclose other of Pedro's mine and treasure locations as it has already located the mine discovered in 1940.

29. I had long suspected the existence of this mine since my finding of the Peralta master map and disclosed its approximate position over a year previous to its discovery in "TRAIL OF THE LOST DUTCHMAN," published February 1939.

30. Many such signs I have seen, followed and photographed, not only in the Superstitions but in other places throughout the West and Mexico. From California to Missouri they are cut, scratched or laid out upon the ground with stones. But always their import is the same; they are traveling or location directions to something which was considered of value at the time they were made. If you come across any, let me in on the secret please!

31. The only light or reflection sign which I have seen so far in the Superstitions was that of a triangle sign reflected onto a cliff face in LaBarge Canyon about three miles above its Boulder Canyon junction. This occurred August 6, 1937 at about 2:00 P.M. and shown for approximately ten minutes.

32. Such superstitions caused by natural enough means have been the chief reason why Indians have refused to divulge the mines locations even though it is believed that certain Apaches still living know the approximate sites of the mines which they covered. Geronimo's gold, also located in the Superstitions is another example, for though his nephew, Chief Grey Horse, is still alive and living meagerly upon a government pension, he will not make any effort to obtain it for himself or divulge its site. In more recent years of course the mines and treasures which the Apaches hid during pioneer days are kept secret from white men simply because the locations are not upon a reservation and the Indians have learned by sad experience that they would be very unlikely to profit from such disclosures.

33. This marker was discovered by myself in the presence of George Snell and Francis Splichal June 28, 1937 because both had seen one of the stones in the cactus and had reported it as an axhead. As originally found it contained only the west and southeast pointers. A naturalist's opinion, based upon the growth rate of the cactus around the stones, placed the date of their insertion at approximately ninety years ago during the Peralta period.

34. Compass declination refers to the position of magnetic north to which the compass needle points in relation to the position of true north which never changes. Declination for the year 1847 is 12 degrees 58 minutes east, and for the year 1944, 14 degrees, 16 minutes east. Because of this difference direction lines and pointers may be dated to the year in which they were laid out by compass, and treasure hunters following them today by compass would be considerably mislead.

35. There seem to be two possibilities for the southeast and west pointers. One is that they are pointing out further clues or signs which have not yet been found. The other is that they were purposely made to confuse anyone who might stumble upon the marker and actually have no significance otherwise.

36. I have never personally seen these arrastres though I took unusual care in interviewing many pioneer travelers over the Apache Trail who said that they had seen them as described. Apparently the location of this first camp when the three brothers were together is different from that established later by Pedro when he returned from Chihuahua City for Tex Barkley tells of a mile further up river near the back end of Mesquite Flat about the remains of a stone-built house, a corral upon a nearby mesa also fenced in by stones, and of two more arrastres which he had first seen decades ago while riding range. From this location the course of travel into the mountains would have been over Mesquite and Tortilla Flats and back over the pass from Tortilla Flat into LaBarge Canyon and then as before.

37. This crosscut or narrow prospecting trench, cut steplike into solid rock, was accidently found by myself and Johnathan Burbridge while we were ourselves prospecting up Bluff Springs Mountain for the source of the gold in hemitite found during November 1938. The gold and the crosscut are both located upon the Whiz Bang Mining Claims which I recorded (Book 50 of Mines) in Florence, Pinal County.

38. Found by Johnathan Burbridge and Norman Barton in Needle Canyon during November 1938.

39. So much can be deduced from the Apaches' own accounts of having covered the mines, and from the now known locations of quartz or quartzite veins in the region which all assay some gold content where they are exposed. Intrusives in this region are of Tertiary age or earlier where exposed and local pre-mineralization faulting is intense and complicated making it geologically possible for shoots of rich

intensely mineralized ore to exist in the larger, low-grade masses upon the site of which the hidden shafts would be located. Both local geological and mineralogical clues may be obtained by a careful study of "ARIZONA LODE GOLD MINES AND GOLD MINING" issued by the Arizona Bureau Of Mines, University of Arizona, Tucson. It might be pointed out, too, that Pedro Peralta never had the opportunity to map or otherwise disclose, except by locally marked out signs, the sites of his later discoveries; and even the Apaches who covered these additional mines which are not recorded by Peralta family tradition, would not know where he hid the results of over a year's production from them!

40. Found by George Snell in the presence of myself and Francis Splichal. Later I had it identified as the hand-made type still common in the back country of Mexico. Thus does bonanza history backtrail itself!

41. The exact site was first shown to me in the presence of George Snell and Francis Splichal by Abe Reid July 1937.

42. Tex Barkley several times detailed to me how he had come upon the ruins of this house thirty-odd years ago in one of the arroyos at the foot of Weaver's Needle. When he, himself, fifteen years after became interested in hunting for the lost mines, he went back to it for clues but found in the meantime that someone had dismantled it rock for rock and scattered the rocks. This some local people attribute it to Apaches who were afraid the house would serve as a clue to the covered mines.

43. This charcoal pit is perhaps the best evidence of nearby mining. It was discovered by myself January 29, 1938 in the presence of Walt Upson, Hubert D'Autremont and Gene Holman and contained layers of ashes and charcoal down to a depth of three feet. By laying a wind chute of earthed-up stones to it much the same effect could be obtained as that created by the bellows upon a blacksmith's forge.

44. I established the massacre site exactly by finding there one of Silverlock's claim notices after local inquiry had elicited the information that many bones, Spanish relics and the lucky treasure had all been found there through the years. Some evidence of his widespread digging still exists near the cliffs.

45. I am indebted to Abe Reid for most of this information which he had obtained first hand from the Apache involved himself.

46. I finally discovered this marker November 23, 1938 in the presence of Johnathan Burbridge after one of my photographs had disclosed its presence. Detailed examination showed that it had been cleverly chiseled to give the shape wanted and had been hoisted up and chocked into place.

47. This was a man named Williamson, who wrote a letter published some years ago in the Phoenix newspaper.

48. Norman Barton, member of my second 1938 expedition, obtained this information first hand from Mart Charlebois, then of Glendale, Arizona, and relayed it to me by letter.

49. Personally related to me by Abe Reid during July 1937 in the presence of George Snell and Francis Splichal.

50. Where then is the gold which never left the Superstitions?

51. I am indebted to Reinhart Petrasch of Globe for much of this data which he had himself, obtained from The Dutchman during his youth. Reported in the Arizona Republic of February 5, 1943: "R. Petrasch, 75 years old, shot and killed himself at the city barns yesterday afternoon. A note indicated he had killed himself because of failing eyesight. Last Monday he had gone to Clyde Shute, Justice of the Peace, and had a statement prepared. The statement said: "I am now 75. I was born in Germany May 21, 1867, and came to the United States when one year old. I am a citizen of the United States. In case of accident or death notify Herman Petrasch in Superior." He had been a rancher and prospector in this county for more than forty years, spending most of his time looking for the Lost Dutchman mine." Perhaps now The Dutchman in the next life will show him the source of the fabulous ore which he couldn't find in this!

52. Gadsden Purchase of 1848, resulting in final occupation of the Mexican-held Southwest by Americans in 1853.

53. As publicly related by Andy Starr himself.

54. The Goldfield deposits, source of the placer gold which had attracted The Dutchman and Wiser, were worked first by C. Hall and D. Sullivan who at the time claimed bonanza ore on and near the surface. Wm. P. Blake in Rept. of Gov. of Ariz., 1898, stated that the mine had then been extensively worked to a depth of 100 feet. Later in 1910 The Young Mines Company acquired the property, making an unknown fabulous production variously estimated by miners then working there as around a million dollars, after which to the year 1925 $67,000 was produced from extensive development work. Ariz. Lode Gold Mines and Gold Mining, Bulletin No. 137, Arizona Bureau of Mines, details known history and production.

55. Erected by The Dons, a Phoenix businessmens club, who formerly conducted for benefit of tourists a one day picnic "trek" to the southern slopes of the Superstitions.

56. Errosion of the Goldfield deposits and the breaking down of numerous stringer veins in the vicinity was the source of this placer gold.

57. A composite of local memory gathered first by Tom Weeden while he was proposing the partnership search with J. D. Walker.

58. Roy Bradford discovered this cache, and personally pointed out its location and detailed its contents ot me in the presence of George Snell and Francis Splichal, July 1937, though he had himself failed to identify it. Portable coffee mills or hand grinders were commonly carried at the time because coffee was then sold only in bulk form, and the square iron nails were replaced in common use during the

late seventies by the wire nail of today, unmistakeably dating the cache to The Dutchman's time. And no one at that time except the itinerent carpenter, Wiser, was in the Superstitions during the early seventies who would have been normally carrying around assorted nails in his kit.

59. Related to me personally on several different occasions by Carl Clark.

60. Blevins entirely missed the point of his father's little adventure, about which he often told—for it points to the region of The Dutchman's bonanza mine from still another direction. In fact, if all the men who had attempted to follow The Dutchman had been as accurate about the point at which they lost the trail, the mine would long since have been localized to a definite area and probably found.

61. George McClarty often himself told of this sanguine adventure, and after The Dutchman's death, his tale was published in (date now unknown) The Arizona Star in Tucson, setting off many searches.

62. A. L. Pellegrin related these details to Abe Reid who repeated them to me.

63. Such details are so necessary as clues that after obtaining them from Reinhart Petrasch I took great pains to verify them from others too numerous to list who had either heard Julia Thomas repeat them or who intimately knew someone who had. They are as exact as I could contrive from this composite of first, second and third hand information.

64. In 1939 I interviewed "Grandmother" Henshaw who was The Dutchman's landlady. She has forgotten more of him than most of the present-day "historians" ever knew.

65. Julia Thomas wasn't a bit secretive about these things then or afterwards.

66. This earthquake of which I could find no record beyond local tradition, occurred because of major faults underlying the Superstitions near Phoenix and the Santa Catalinas near Tucson and seems to have expended its force in these mountains. It was described as very severe by most old residents, and as far south as Tucson it is said that no mountains could be seen for three days after because of the resulting dust haze. To this day in the Superstitions I and many others have heard the distant rumbling which indicates that movements are still occurring along the faults, according to geologists.

67. Records of this flood and of Jacob Walz's death may be found in the files of the present Phoenix Gazette, Phoenix, Arizona.

68. This first stone face is located about three-fourths of a mile south of First Water Ranch, along the trail which today follows the easiest way toward West Boulder Canyon. I finally located it December, 1941.

69. Exact dates cannot be obtained because of removal of Fort McDowel records to the archives of the War Department in Washington. However, 1876 would be exact within a year or so in the opinion of numerous local people who remembered the mild excitement caused by Dr. Thorne.

70. It has often been argued that Indians did not know the locations of mineral wealth since they rarely engaged in mining and never in mining requiring the extraction of metal from rock. This is true, but only until white men had found the sources of gold and silver! And since this finding was invariably the cause of actual discomfort if not real danger to the Indians themselves they afterwards were very well informed indeed, and still are! The latest of many communications which I have received on this point is a letter dated January 25, 1945 from Perry J. Sherman of Hot Springs, Arkansas, who had befriended Geronimo's nephew, Chief Grey Horse, whom he quotes: "One night we were talking about old Fort Apache and vicinity which I had visited several times, and I told him (Chief Grey Horse) I had often wondered about the gold in the Superstitions and he said: "No, there are several mines hidden there. Geronimo told me all about them." It must be remembered that the Indian's principle method of recording things was by word of mouth, from one to another, father to son, tribe to tribe.

71. Charles G. Mason sold out his interest to Colonel James M. Barney of Yuma whose son, James M. Barney, published in Arizona Municipalities a comprehensive article about the detailed history of the fabulous Silver King Mine and of the ghost towns of Silver King and Picket Post or Pinal which the mine once supported. An excellent reportage of first-hand history in the making, the more amazing because true. Detailed data on the actual mining may be obtained in Geology and Ore Deposits Of The Superior Mining Area, Arizona, Bulletin No. 151 of the Arizona Bureau of Mines.

72. I discovered this shell myself in the presence of John Vall, June 12, 1937, and one of the best pieces of detective work which I have done in the Superstitions. And Vall, of course, is not his real name.

73. Jack Frazer, who was no amateur miner himself as witness his Iron King Mining Claim located March 17, 1942 shortly before his death and recorded at Florence, Book 52 of Mines, gave me personally in August 1937 the true story of the two ex-soldiers whom he had closely questioned and whose gold ore he had actually seen so many years before. He also referred me to the Mason family, then of San Francisco, who had, he said, the early Silver King Mine records.

74. I have promised not to name them though after much persuasion I saw one of the letters. There are others besides myself who would like to go lost mine hunting just this once!

75. Russell Perkins, postmaster of Tortilla Flat, in 1943 and again during January 1945, personally told me this. The campsite is still there!

76. Roy Bradford related this to me in the presence of George Snell and Francis Splichal during August 1937 without in the least realizing its significance. But such is treasure hunters' luck!

77. J. J. Carrol of Los Angeles, personally gave me this account of both his father's and his own good —and bad—fortune when I interviewed him at his home during December 1937.

78. The spring is there in LaBarge Canyon two miles above its Boulder Canyon junction! It is a permanent spring, probably fed through an east-west fault through here, and which, incidently, was responsible for the mineralization which Carrol encountered nearby.

79. During a very charming evening at his home in 1942 Charlie Morgan related this to me among other things.

80. Garden Valley is about three-fourths of a mile east-northeast of First Water Ranch.

81. The Apache tradition of the silver "Antelope" is doubtless due to the errosion-cut shapes of silver ore which seem to be alternately exposed and hidden by flood debris somewhere in the bed of Queen Creek. It rmains to be seen whether this is actually the "mountain of silver" described by David Hawkins' uncle. Hawkins intends to find out! See note 82.

82. David Hawkins himself wrote me of this from his home in Alma, Illinois in a letter dated October 26, 1942. Quotations are exact. And the fabulous Silver King Mine in the same region lends considerable weight to the alluring possibility!

83. Tex Barkley, owner of the Quarter-Circle-U Ranch and former employer of McDonald, related this to me during June 1937.

84. Often related by Fred Mullins himself according to a composite of local memory.

85. Ray Howland told me this one evening in October 1938 while we were yarning at the little cabin he then owned on the southern slopes of the Superstitions.

86. The posse which finally located Ruth's remains January 8, 1932, was headed by Deputy Sheriff Jeff Adams and included W. A. "Tex" Barkley, Hassie Cline, Ace Gardener and Gabriel Robles.

87. I had to "composite" these details from numerous persons with whom Ruth came into contact upon his arrival in Arizona.

88. I could make an excellent guess but dare not in public print. I suspect also that others could too!

89. Tex Barkley himself told me this—and it was verified by his neighbors.

90. Abe Reid, who had himself obtained the information directly from Purnell and Keenan while working for First Water Ranch, furnished me these facts July 1937 in the presence of George Snell and Francis Splichal. However, additional information has just reached me in a letter dated February 13, 1945 from Walter G. Armeson of Montpelier, Idaho, which I quote in part: "I met Purnell in 1934 on Leon Creek, he had just rode into that country from Arizona . . . told me about this man Ruth getting lost. Purnell said he found the skull but did not mention any bullet hole or having been hired to pack for Ruth. Purnell said his camp was only one-fourth mile from Ruth's camp."

91. I have seen the tracks, and have been both trailed and shot at. But I have done a little tracking myself!

92. I informed Erwin Ruth of the marker's discovery and in return received more information that Ruth suspects he gave me.

93. Harvey Mott of the Arizona Republic was there and wrote much of this for his paper and later reviewed my booklet, "Trail Of The Lost Dutchman." But as I told him in 1939 when I publicly reported facts at variance with his observations—and must do so again—that things were not what they seemed. Finding the skull was an accident, and Ruth's remains should not have been where they were found unless they had been carried there by someone then in the mountains. Therefore, and while Mott's observations were accurate, it was really those other things seen only by the trailwise eyes of experienced mountain men which tell the whole truth and offer clue to the identity of our unnamed "Mr. X."

94. I found this bottle myself March 5, 1942. Had not war intervened I might have had this treasure trail unraveled by now.

95. "LOST DUTCHMAN MINE HUNTERS WILL TRY OUT RADIO LOCATOR," was the headline. I quote: "Armed with a radio locator which he hopes will be just what is needed to wrest the secret of the famous Lost Dutchman gold mine from the Arizona hills, Barry Storm, author and adventurer, visited San Diego yesterday en route to start his fourth expedition after the almost legendary gold workings." And I thought Jenkins had it! Indeed, it was the accident of his death that caused me at the time to use that same radio locator in finding the Lost Peralta mine instead.